COL

C

CHINA

Christina Donaldson

Consultant: Janine Evans,
Stoke-on-Trent
City Museum and Art Gallery

HarperCollins*Publishers*

HarperCollins Publishers
PO Box, Glasgow G4 0NB

First published 1997

Reprint 10 9 8 7 6 5 4 3 2 1 0

All of the illustrations in this book have been supplied courtesy of Sotheby's in London, with the exception of:
Page 75: courtesy of Wedgwood; page 157: courtesy of Stoke-on-Trent City Museum and Art Gallery; page 203: courtesy of Paul Knight.

ISBN 0 00 471009 6

Created and produced by Flame Tree Publishing, part of
The Foundry Creative Media Co. Ltd
The Long House, Antrobus Rd, Chiswick, London W4 5HY

Special thanks to John Dunne, and to photographers Glyn Clarkson and Paul Kinchin

Printed in Italy by Amadeus S.p.A.

Contents

Staffordshire jug, c.1820

Introduction

Everyone owns a piece of China. Old or new, pottery or porcelain, patterned or plain, functional or decorative, there will be at least one ceramic item in your household about which you would like to know more. The usual questions are: Is it old? Where was it made? Who made it? How is it decorated? What is it made from? What is it for? and, of course, What is it worth?

This book is an essential guide to all types of European pottery and porcelain made since the middle ages, and it is designed both to introduce a complete beginner to the subject and to interest and aid a seasoned collector. With this book, you will be able to correctly identify any mystery object, and armed with that basic information, go ahead with more detailed research, and perhaps eventually establish its value.

There are seven key sections in the book, and each is designed to stand alone – to dip into – or to read as part of a comprehensive introduction to this fascinating subject. The first two sections detail the different types of ceramic body and the various methods of decoration, which, once identified, can provide clues to the date and place of production.

The third section looks at the various shapes of ware produced, and discusses function and methods of production. Next is a short section devoted to the influence on ware from outside Europe, and from other disciplines. The fifth section takes a more historical approach, discussing style chronologically, and giving brief histories of the more important or commonly found Continental and English makers. This section will be helpful if the maker of the piece is known, or the style is distinctive to its period.

The last two sections look at the field of ceramics from a rather different angle, the first examining collectable items which may not have been covered elsewhere, and the second looking at aspects of collecting and identification. There are a great deal of valuable tips for dating, identifying restoration and repair and hints

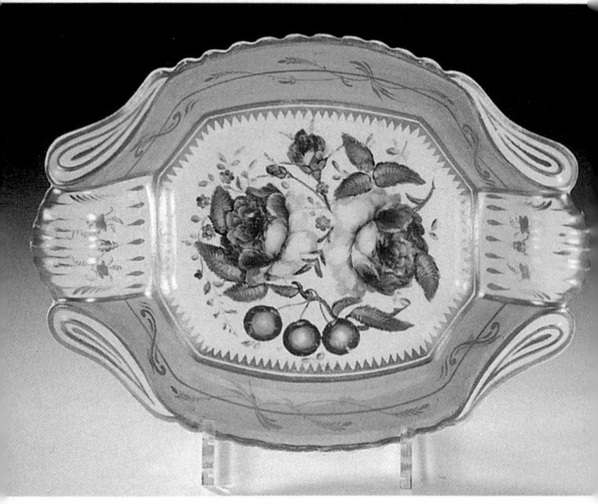

English porcelain dessert dish, c.1830

on buying and selling, as well as a brief chapter on factory marks.

The correct identification of a ceramic object can be extremely satisfying, but also very frustrating. It is important to keep an open mind and not make any assumptions about a piece. Great age does not necessarily mean high value or rarity, as many ceramic pieces were, and still are, mass produced. Look at the piece from the various angles described above, use the information in this book, and, with a little luck you may be rewarded.

Whieldon-type creamware teapot, c.1760

How To Use This Book

This book details a wide variety of information about European pottery and porcelain – everything from types of ware and decoration, through to methods of production, shapes, influences from other countries, and styles and movements across history.

The book is divided into six sections, together with a Compendium at the end.

Each part is colour-coded for easy reference. Part One, which appears in soft green, presents general information about types of ware, including porcelain, earthenware, pearlware, ironstone and many others. Part Two is colour-coded pink, and provides facts about the various types of decoration, from underglaze, through to surface-painted decoration, printed decoration and other decorative techniques. Part Three discusses form and function, including the many different shapes, and methods of production, and is coded blue. Part Four, all about influences from around the world, is coded yellow. Part Five, coded lilac, presents an in-depth investigation of European porcelain and pottery throughout history – from the Middle Ages, through Art Nouveau and Art Deco, to the present day. There is an interesting section on factories, designers and movements, all of which have had a profound influence on china over the years. Part Six, coded a deep green, contains key information about collecting including facts about limited editions, Toby and character jugs, nursery ware and miniatures, as well as commemorative wares, animals and novelty items.

The Compendium contains general information about porcelain and pottery including material about dating, fakes, forgeries, pricing, and buying at auction, as well as a unique section on antique marks, and how to form a collection. You'll also learn the essentials in care and restoration of china. There is a handy list of addresses of various helpful organizations, and a Glossary explaining terms which might be unfamiliar. At the end of the book you'll find an index which lists every subject and type of china found in this book.

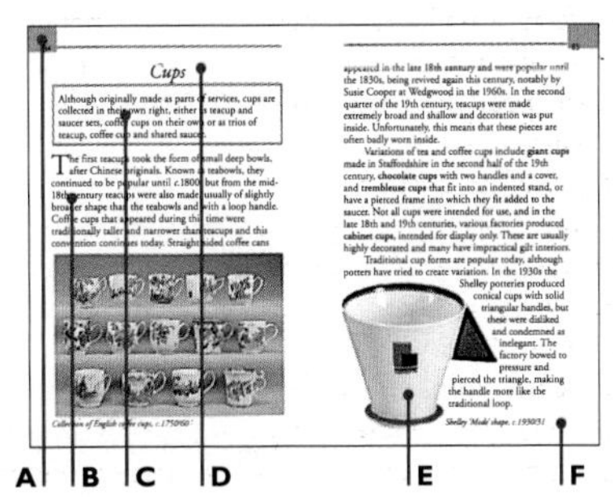

Cups

Although originally made as parts of services, cups are collected in their own right, either as teacup and saucer sets, coffee cups on their own or as trios of teacup, coffee cup and shared saucer.

The first teacups took the form of small deep bowls, after Chinese originals. Known as teabowls, they continued to be popular until *c.*1800 but from the mid-18th-century teacups were also made usually of slightly broader shape than the teabowls and with a loop handle. Coffee cups that appeared during this time were traditionally taller and narrower than teacups and this convention continues today. Straight-sided coffee cans appeared in the late 18th century and were popular until the 1830s, being revived again this century, notably by Susie Cooper at Wedgwood in the 1960s. In the second quarter of the 19th century, teacups were made extremely broad and shallow and decoration was put inside. Unfortunately, this means that these pieces are often badly worn inside.

Variations of tea and coffee cups include **giant cups** made in Staffordshire in the second half of the 19th century, **chocolate cups** with two handles and a cover, and **trembleuse cups** that fit into an indented stand, or have a pierced frame into which they fit added to the saucer. Not all cups were intended for use, and in the late 18th and 19th centuries, various factories produced **cabinet cups**, intended for display only. These are usually highly decorated and many have impractical gilt interiors.

Traditional cup forms are popular today, although potters have tried to create variation. In the 1930s the Shelley potteries produced conical cups with solid triangular handles, but these were disliked and condemned as inelegant. The factory bowed to pressure and pierced the triangle, making the handle more like the traditional loop.

Shelley 'Mode' shape, c.1930/31

A B C D E F

A The page number appears in a colour-coded box which indicates which part you are in.

B Essential information about the subject appears in a concise and fascinating introductory passage.

C A unique box details key facts from the information which appears on this page.

D The title of the chapter, in this case Cups, which are one of the shapes discussed, appears at the beginning of every new section.

E The topic covered on these pages will be illustrated with clear photographs.

F A short caption explains the photographs that appear on this page.

TYPES OF WARE 

Introduction

The first section of this book attempts to cover in some detail the many varied types of wares which make up European ceramics. The term ceramics is a general one, so for the purposes of this book and to aid initial identification 'ceramics' as a whole can be divided into two types.

Earthenware: Fired to a temperature of up to 1200°C. Porous, and therefore is generally glazed on the surface to render it non-porous.
Porcelain: Fired to a temperature of 1250°C–1400°C and above. Hard, non-porous and translucent.

The different types of ware use different clays in their composition, and it is the type and colour of the basic clay which gives the ware its distinguishing features. In particular, earthenware, which is also sometimes called pottery, appears in many different forms, all of which, along with their distinguishing features will be examined.

The composition of the ware is not simply made from clay as it is dug from the ground, but from a recipe of clay mixed with other materials in small quantities. The details of each recipe were usually unique to a particular potter or manufacturer and were closely guarded secrets. Some of these types of 'recipes' will be explained in more detail in subsequent chapters.

Hint: The most straightforward way to tell porcelain from earthenware is to hold an item up to a light and check to see if light passes through – this is known as the translucency test. If the piece is translucent, it will appear to glow, with a pale orange or green colour, and something moved behind the piece, your finger, for instance, will create a shadow.

Demonstrating translucency: a hand seen through a bone china plate

Porcelain

Porcelain can be grouped into two types:
Hard paste, or true porcelain, is made up of kaolin (china clay) and petuntze (a variety of feldspar called china stone), and is fired to a temperature of at least 1350°C–1400°C.
Soft paste, or artificial porcelain, contains a mixture of white clay and ground glass, fired to a temperature of approximately 1100°C.

Porcelain is basically a hard, translucent non-porous ware. There are some important variations in the recipes used by different factories which result in some variation in appearance, and these are useful to understand when trying to identify or attribute a piece of porcelain.

Porcelain first appeared in China, and developed over a period of several thousand years. It was only when exports from China began to appear in Europe that potters attempted to recreate the hard translucent body from which Oriental porcelains were made, and it was not until the 18th century that they were truly successful.

Other ingredients were then added by particular factories to create their own unique recipes.

Hard paste porcelain was first developed by Johan Frederich Böttger at Meissen *c.*1710. Most other German and European factories followed suit in developing a hard paste body and most modern continental porcelains are of a hard paste type.

A type of **soft paste** porcelain was first developed

Meissen hard paste porcelain coffee pot, c.1730

by the Medici in Italy in the mid- to late-16th century, although these wares were experimental and short-lived. In the early 18th century the two main areas of soft paste porcelain development and use were France and England. At this time it was thought that the translucency of porcelain came from the addition of ground glass to the body, however, this was not the case.

Kaolin, the necessary ingredient of true porcelain, was not discovered in France until 1768. After this date French potters made the two types of body in tandem, with the hard paste gradually taking over by the beginning of the 19th century.

In England, the first experimental porcelain factories appeared in the 1740s.

Although initially using ground glass like the France potters, two factories – Lowestoft and Bow – began adding bone ash to their recipes. This enabled the body to withstand higher kiln temperatures without collapsing. At Bristol and Worcester, steatite or soapstone was added, creating a body which was more durable and able to withstand changes in temperature without crazing, necessary when the wares were mainly for tea- and coffee-making!

Worcester sauce boat, c.1754

True hard paste porcelain was produced briefly in England by William Cookworthy at Plymouth from 1768, and at New Hall in Staffordshire in the 1780s.

Towards the end of the 18th century and the beginning of the 19th century, more and more English factories were using a larger amount of bone ash in their recipes and this ware can strictly speaking be called **bone china.** Today, the term 'bone china' has connotations of quality and translucency which we associate with modern English porcelain, but in fact the basic recipe has been used since the early 19th century.

CHARACTERISTICS

Hard paste

- Hard, glassy appearance.
- White or grey-tinted colour.
- Brittle chips tend to have a ridged, flaked appearance like a chip on glass.
- Cracks tend to be fine and straight.

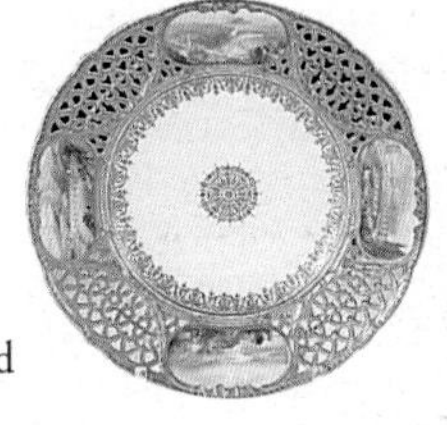

Coalport bone china plate, c.1900

Soft paste

- Creamy or soft white colour.
- Chips tend to have a crumbly appearance.
- Cracks are often crooked or curving.
- Bone china tends to be white and is prone to crazing and discoloration.

Biscuit porcelain

Although most porcelains were lead-glazed, the body could be left unglazed. In this state it is known as biscuit or bisque porcelain. Biscuit porcelain was frequently used for the production of figures, notably at Sèvres in the late 18th and 19th centuries, and at Derby and Minton in England in the late 18th and early 19th centuries. Because the ware was fired only once and was unglazed it was possible to retain much more detail, hence its popularity for figure production.

During the late 19th century, in France and Germany particularly, bisque porcelain figures were mass produced in large quantities, often with coloured surface decoration (coloured bisque). These wares are of relatively poor quality and survive in large numbers today. Bisque was also used for making dolls' heads and bodies in the late 19th century. These can be of quite fine quality and are very collectable.

- Soft paste biscuit tends to have a white hue and soft crumbly appearance.
- Hard paste biscuit is grey and the edges are harder and more angular.

The following pages describe two further variations of porcelain, both particularly Victorian phenomena.

Continental mass-produced coloured bisque figure, c.1890

Parian ware

Type: Biscuit porcelain, generally unglazed.
Use: Mostly decorative wares, vases, figures and busts.
Date of production: *c.*1840–1900. **Where produced:** Staffordshire, England. Notably Copeland, Minton, Wedgwood. Belleek in Ireland also used a parian-type ware as their main body, usually glazed.

Parian ware is a type of unglazed biscuit porcelain of creamy colour, similar in appearance to marble. It was developed simultaneously by Minton and Copeland in the 1840s as a material suitable for the reproduction of marble figures. The term 'parian' derives from the name of the Greek island of Paros, famed for its quarries of fine white marble. The ware was perfected by the late 1840s and was produced by a number of English factories. It enabled 'sculpture' to be produced on a large scale and meant that the average middle-class family could afford to buy what appeared to be an original sculpture at a fraction of the normal cost.

Reproductions were made not only of classical Greek and Roman works, but also of contemporary sculpture. Subjects included politicians, sportsmen and royalty, as well as animals and a wide range of contemporary interpretations of classical subjects. Although usually left undecorated, parian could be coloured and gilded. Some factories produced lesser-quality coloured figures. but Minton produced items of stunning quality with the selective use of coloured enamel and gilding.

Parian was used in a limited way for useful wares such as jugs and vases; however, when left unglazed the matt surface tended to pick up dirt and could retain a grubby appearance. Many parian busts and figures were originally displayed under glass domes for this reason.

English parian ware bust of Apollo, c.1860

Pâte-sur-pâte

Type: Parian ware with layers of slip decoration. Lead-glazed. **Use:** Decorative wares.
Date of production: *c.*1860 in France, *c.*1870 to the present day in England. Recently revived at Minton.
Where produced: France, notably Sèvres; Staffordshire, notably Minton. Also at a number of other factories in both countries, often of lower quality.

Pâte-sur-pâte (pronounced *pat-sur-pat* and literally meaning 'paste-on-paste') was a technique developed at the Sèvres factory in France. It involves the building of a design from layer upon layer of thin translucent slip, finely tooled to create a shallow relief cameo effect. The slip decoration can be tinted any colour, but is often white over a coloured ground, usually blue, olive green, brown or salmon pink.

The greatest exponent of this art was Marc Louis Solon who came to Minton from Sèvres in 1870. He and his pupils, notably Alboine Birks (who continued to work until 1937), produced a large quantity of high quality ware. Pâte-sur-pâte was a complicated technique and all pieces are highly sought after, the larger ones often fetching extremely high prices.

English pâte-sur-pâte decorated vase, c.1870

Earthenware

The differences between earthenware and porcelain have already been identified. Earthenware comes in even more guises than porcelain and the following sections will discuss each type in turn, giving a technical description and hints on identifying, and providing examples of the various factories which have produced the different wares, and at what period. This information is invaluable, especially since many of these wares are unmarked, and the factories which produced them unrecorded.

Do not despair if the type of ware to be identified does not specifically appear in this book. Many 19th- and 20th-century wares are made from a hybrid body developed from these early types of earthenware. Modern earthenwares are opaque, white or cream with a neutral coloured glaze, which often has a tendency to craze.

More recently, factories have favoured a stronger stoneware-type body which will withstand the heat of a domestic oven. So-called oven-to-table wares are now the norm for everyday use, and some of these earlier services, such as those made by Denby in the 1950s and 1960s, are either still in use or avidly collected. Such wares can often be distinguished by their matt glaze and rather grainy surface appearance.

Wemyss earthenware pig, c.1900

Slipware

Type: Low fired earthenware. Surface slip decoration. Lead-glazed. **Use:** In the 17th and 18th centuries, generally for useful wares, some highly decorative. In the 19th and 20th centuries, popular with studio and craft potters. **Date of production:** 17th century to present day. **Where produced:** England and elsewhere in northern Europe.

Slip is a mixture of clay and water which is used to decorate a usually reddish or brown earthenware body. The decorative effect is achieved by the patterns made with the slip and by the contrasts of colour, usually shades of yellow, brown and ochre. The item would then be covered in a non-porous lead glaze.

Slipware was produced in large quantities in Staffordshire in the 17th and 18th centuries, with items such as simple baking dishes through to complex chargers and jugs, often decorated with naive figures and embroidery-like patterns. Pieces can be dated, but these must be treated with care, as many objects made by art potters in the 19th century bear spurious 17th- or 18th-century dates. Pieces can also be inscribed with the name of a particular owner or potter, and sometimes bear incised inscriptions. Decoration can be applied or moulded in relief, trailed (a similar technique to piping icing on a cake), combed, marbled and incised. Incised decoration is known as 'sgraffito'.

A rare and collectable piece of slipware might

employ a combination of these types of decoration along with a date and name. Slipwares are the earliest examples in England of relatively sophisticated, decorative rather than purely functional wares.

Staffordshire slipware dish, c.1700

Delft

Type: Earthenware. Tin-glazed. Blue and white or polychrome decoration. **Use:** All types of ware, useful and decorative. **Date of production:** Early 16th–19th century in Holland. In England, *c.*1650–1780. **Where produced:** Holland and England, where it is known as Delftware. (Note: other European tin-glazed earthenwares are discussed under Maiolica.)

So-called Delft or Delftwares were the earliest attempts by Dutch, and later English, potters to emulate the fine blue and white porcelains being imported into Europe from China and Japan by Dutch and Portuguese traders. The name Delft comes from the town in Holland which was a major centre of production for these new wares.

The potters attempted to simulate the white body of the Oriental porcelain wares by covering their soft earthenwares in a thick lead glaze made opaque by the addition of tin-oxide. The blue, and later polychrome decoration, was painted on to the surface of the thick unfired glaze using metal oxides to achieve different colours, notably cobalt for blue. The colours fused into the glaze when fired. Although initially Oriental-style patterns and shapes were popular, Delftwares can also be decorated in a very classical European style with subjects often derived from contemporary engravings. Powdered manganese was also used as a ground colour, giving a mottled purple appearance when fired. White enamel painted on to the surface over a blue or greyish ground is known as 'bianco-sopra-bianco'.

Hint: Delftwares and all tin-glazed earthenwares are easily identified by the thick opaque glaze which has a tendency to chip along the edge of the object. These chips are similar in appearance to chips on an old enamel plate.

Small chips on the edge of Delftware were often present from new and do not necessarily harm the value or aesthetic appearance of a piece. Beware of late 19th and 20th century Dutch imitations of Delftware which have 'Delft' inscribed on the base. Although mainly decorated in blue and white, these are often not true Delft tin-glazed wares, but ordinary lead-glazed earthenwares made for a mass market in Delft style.

Dutch Delft vase, c.1700

Rim of Delft plate with chips to edge

Maiolica

Type: Low-fired earthenware. Tin-glazed. **Use:** All types of ware. **Date of production:** 15th century to present day. **Where produced:** Italy, Spain, Germany, France and other European countries. Known as faience in France and Germany, Delft in Holland and England.

The term maiolica comes from Majorca on the Balearic Islands, through which the first tin-glazed earthenwares were imported into Italy. These wares came mainly from Spain where a tradition of lustre-decorated tin-glazed earthenware dates back to the 10th or 11th centuries. Tin-glazed earthenwares were, in fact, made all over Europe, deriving originally from the Eastern Islamic countries. In Italy, this type of ware became extremely popular in the 16th and 17th centuries.

Decoration of the wares in Italy, Spain and France was quite different from northern Europe, with cobalt blue being far less widely used. The tendency in Spain was for lustre decoration which will be discussed separately. French wares used sparse, polychrome colours in a tradition which continues today in the native pottery of the various regions. In Italy, the use of strong colours was preferred and the designs are often dense, covering the entire piece. Lustre glazes were also popular, influenced by the imported wares from Spain. The use of tin-glazed earthenware continues today in most Mediterranean countries, the wares being distinguished by a thick white glaze and a reddish or pale coloured body.

Rouen (French) faience ewer, 18th century

Stoneware

Type: High temperature fired earthenware. Non-porous. Salt or lead-glazed. **Use:** All types of ware, but particularly useful items. **Date of production:** Late medieval period to present day.
Where used: Northern Europe, particularly Germany and England. After the late 18th century it was used in Germany mainly for 'native'-type wares, in England by art potters and, more recently, by studio potters.

Stoneware is made from clays which can be fired at high temperatures (1200°C–1350°C), causing the particles of the body to fuse together, giving a granular, hard, stone-like appearance from which the name of the ware derives. Although strictly speaking stoneware does not require a glaze due to its non-porous properties, it is usually glazed, occasionally with a lead glaze but more commonly with a salt glaze.

Salt glazes are quite literally made when common salt is thrown into the kiln during firing, where it combines with aluminium and silica in the clay to form a thin, but hard surface glaze. During this process hydrochloric acid gas is given off, which is both poisonous and corrosive, part of the reason why salt-glazed stonewares were mass produced for only a relatively short period. The term stoneware can be applied to several various types of ware, some of which will be discussed in more detail.

In England the production of stoneware was

perfected by a potter called John Dwight, working in Fulham in the 17th century, and from the early-18th century, the two adjoining counties of Derbyshire and Nottinghamshire also produced salt-glazed stoneware. In Germany the use of stoneware dates back at least to the 13th century. The wares tend to be pale in colour, often beige or grey-blue, and are frequently decorated with underglaze-blue and manganese colours.

Hint: Stonewares can generally be distinguished from earthenware by the dense, grainy appearance of the body and the often 'orange peel' texture of the salt-glaze. Unlike other earthenwares, stoneware can become translucent when a pale body is thinly potted, although it is unlikely to be confused with porcelain, except perhaps with some very early experimental wares.

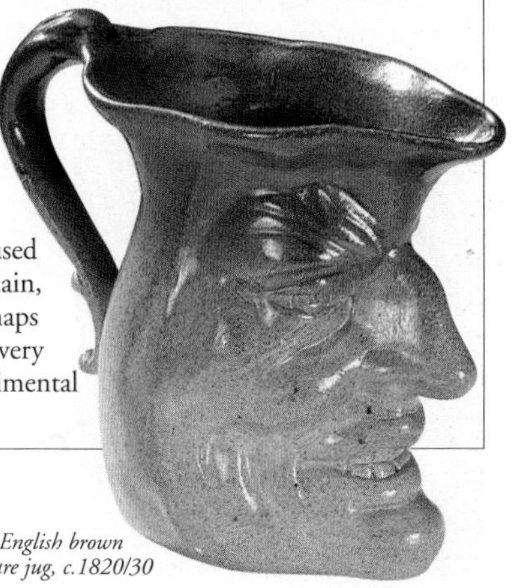

English brown stoneware jug, c.1820/30

White salt-glazed stoneware

Type: High temperature fired earthenware. White. Salt-glazed. **Use:** Useful wares, a small quantity of decorative ware. **Date of production:** *c.*1720–80. **Where produced:** England, notably Staffordshire.

White salt-glazed stoneware has a distinctive white or pale creamy-grey appearance, caused by the ground flint which is added to the clay body before firing. The glaze has a distinctive 'orange peel' texture. Pieces are often very finely pitted and feel extremely light in weight.

The wares can be decorated in a number of ways: polychrome enamelling on the surface in Oriental or European style; or 'scratch blue' decoration where patterns are incised and filled with underglaze-blue colour. Flat wares can also be decorated with moulded panels, produced by pressing them onto metal or stoneware blocks.

Staffordshire white salt-glazed rabbit, c.1750/60

Hollow wares could be cast by pouring the liquid clay slip into the block or mould. Decoration was also sometimes applied to the surface in the form of small pads of clay stamped with a relief pattern.

Most of the items surviving tend to be tea or dinner wares, although there are a number of figures and models of birds, cats and other animals. Pieces may be dated and are sometimes decorated with subjects of a religious or political significance. These pieces and non-table wares tend to be hard to find and are therefore costly.

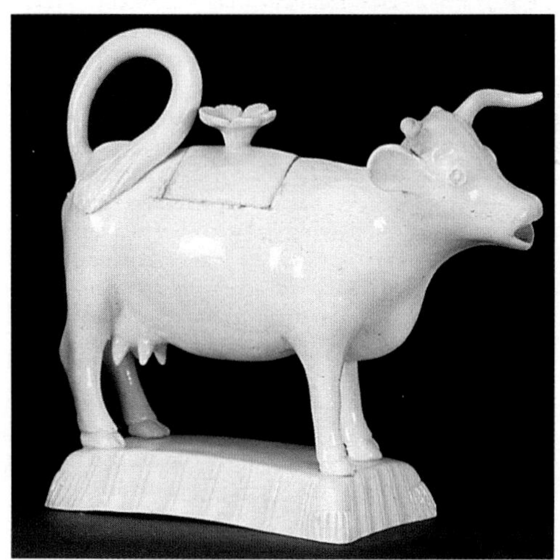

Staffordshire white salt-glazed cow creamer, c.1750/60

Creamware

Type: Fine cream-coloured earthenware, generally covered with a transparent lead glaze. **Use:** Useful wares, some decorative items. **Date of production:** *c.*1750–1800, later revived by Wedgwood and named 'Queensware'. **Where produced:** Staffordshire, Leeds, but also most northern European countries.

Creamware first began to be widely used as an alternative to Delftware in the late 1750s. It was hard and durable, unlike the soft, easily chipped Delftware and was much simpler to produce than white salt-glazed ware. It also had a much smoother glaze. The name most readily associated with creamware is that of Josiah Wedgwood, who in the late 1760s renamed his ware 'Queensware' after gaining the patronage of Queen Charlotte. Besides Staffordshire, the other major centre for the production of creamware was Leeds. Many pieces attributed to Leeds in the past have now been found to derive from a variety of other factories; the ware was produced in most potting areas during the period 1760–80.

The clean-looking body could be painted with coloured enamels or with cobalt blue under the glaze. Alternatively, the ware could be left plain with just simple moulded borders or applied relief or sprigged decoration.

Whieldon is another name associated with creamwares. Thomas Whieldon was a potter in Fenton,

Staffordshire who produced creamwares covered in distinctive coloured glazes. The glazes are normally brown, green, manganese, yellow or blue and are usually dripped or sponged on to the wares, giving a characteristic running or mottled effect. These types of wares are no longer attributed directly to Thomas Whieldon himself as they were also produced elsewhere; however, they do tend to be known as 'Whieldon-type' wares.

Creamwares on the Continent are similar to English examples. They are sometimes impressed with the name of the factory or town where they were produced, as are a small number of English pieces. In Europe, creamware is often known as 'faience fine'.

Creamware teapot, painted decoration, c.1770

Pearlware

Type: Fine pale-coloured earthenware. Lead-glazed. The glaze usually has a blue tint. **Use:** Mainly useful wares, some decorative pieces.
Date of production: *c.*1780–1830. These dates hold for most factories, however the dividing line between true pearlware (and creamware) and ordinary lead-glazed earthenware is sometimes not clear-cut.
Where produced: Staffordshire and other centres in England. Some Continental countries, notably northern Europe. Not as widespread as creamware.

Pearlware is similar to creamware, but is whiter and the clear glaze usually has a faint blue tint (sometimes only visible where the glaze pools, in an impressed mark, for example, or underneath the foot of a piece). It is a durable ware and gradually took over from creamware as the preferred pottery medium. Pearlware was in direct competition with the rapidly improving products of the porcelain manufacturers and there tends to be some similarities between the two, notably in the use of blue and white underglaze decoration.

Until the very early 19th century, in England at least, dinner services, particularly the flat wares, were made almost exclusively in pottery (creamware and pearlware). Early pearlwares tended to be painted with floral or Oriental-style subjects, which gave way to more complex printed decoration in the early 19th century. Spode made extremely high quality printed pearlwares in the early-19th century, and the plates and dishes from their dinner services are now very collectable. Another important manufacturing area for early pearlwares was Liverpool, where pearlware succeeded the declining Delftware industry.

Hint: Distinguishing features of creamware and pearlware:
- Lightweight.
- Very neatly potted, often with a turned appearance to the foot.
- Pale coloured body.
- Creamware glaze appears green where it pools, whereas on pearlware it is grey-blue.

Pearlware (left), creamware (right): colour differences shown under foot

Majolica

Type: Earthenware. Coloured lead-glazed decoration.
Use: Decorative items. Tiles, fountains, garden seats and a limited number of decorative useful wares, such as jugs, game pie dishes, strawberry dishes and teapots.
Date of production: Mid-19th century to *c.*1900.
Where produced: Developed by English factories, notably Minton. Similar wares made by Continental manufacturers in the second half of the 19th century.

The term 'majolica' is an anglicised corruption of 'maiolica' and was a term coined by Minton to describe initially Italian Renaissance-style wares, but which later came to be used for all wares employing coloured glazes to achieve decorative effect.

The wares were frequently moulded or slip cast into elaborate shapes with raised surface decoration which was then highlighted by areas of contrasting coloured glaze. Strong green, white, purple, pink, turquoise and cobalt blue were popular, with the more minor Staffordshire factories and Continental factories using noticeably weaker colours. The main makers in England were

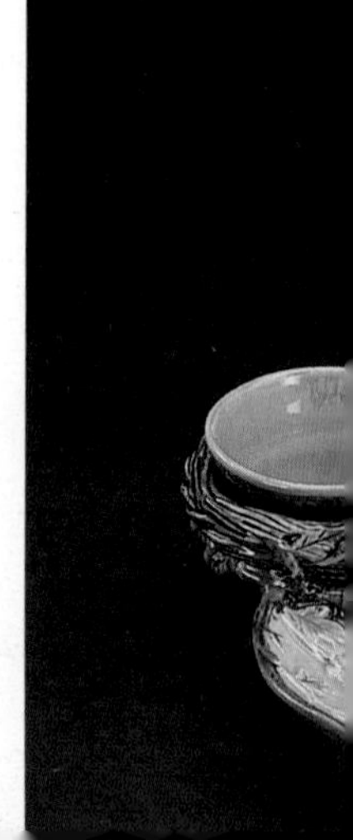

Minton, George Jones, Wedgwood, Copeland, Joseph Holdcroft and William Brownfield. The wares frequently bear impressed or moulded factory marks, although marks can be difficult to decipher as the glaze can pool into them. George Jones' pieces, which can be extremely valuable, often simply bear a pattern number painted in black on to a small glaze-free patch underneath.

Majolica production all but ceased at the beginning of this century, although it had a late flowering at Minton during this period in a range known as 'Secessionist Ware'.

Minton majolica 'monkey' tea set, c.1870

Ironstone

Type: Dense, hard earthenware, containing china-stone. Lead glazed. **Use:** Dinner and dessert wares, some vases and decorative useful wares.
Date of production: Early to late 19th century. Later wares are less obviously 'ironstone' in appearance.
Where produced: England. Makers include Mason's, Spode (stone china), Davenport and Turner.

Ironstone was a type of earthenware developed at the beginning of the 19th century, initially used for making dinner and dessert services. The combination of ingredients used to make the body – the details of which varied from factory to factory – made a strong, durable ware less prone to chipping and cracks than creamware or pearlware.

Various factories produced their own versions; at Spode and Davenport the ware was finely potted and known as 'stone china', other examples bear the marks 'opaque china' or 'semi-porcelain'. Charles and Miles Mason were to become the most prolific makers, and their ware was patented in 1813 under the name 'Mason's Patent Ironstone China'. Naming these wares 'porcelain' and 'china' was somewhat misleading but they were designed to impress the middle-class market at which the wares were aimed. Decoration was often an underglaze-blue printed outline with polychrome enamelling over the top, and patterns were invariably Orientally influenced, as these wares were still competing against Eastern imports. Mason's continues on to the present day under the 'Patent Ironstone' banner, surviving a succession of partnerships and bankruptcies. The ware produced these days has altered in body and appearance.

The most collectable ironstone and stone china wares date from between 1813 and the middle of the 19th century, and include dinner services, very large vases, jugs and pot pourri jars. Mason's even made fire surrounds from ironstone.

Mason's ironstone jug, c.1820

Coloured body wares

The following is a varied group of wares, all distinguished by having distinctive coloured bodies.

Black basalt

Type: Hard, fine stoneware. Owes its dark, black colour to iron and manganese. **Use:** Useful and decorative wares. **Date of production:** Patented by Josiah Wedgwood in 1768. Still produced by Wedgwood today. Popular with other factories *c.*1770–1820. **Where produced:** Staffordshire, England. Some makers in Europe.

So-called black basalt (variously spelled basalte or basaltes) is a hard true stoneware body named after the stone it resembles. It is often left unglazed and either has a velvety matt surface or is polished smooth. Usually decoration is applied or turned, although occasionally pieces can be seen with painted (encaustic) decoration. Wares are rarely marked although Wedgwood and Neale sometimes use impressed marks.

Wedgwood black basalt 'Portland' vase, c.19th century

Jasper ware

Type: Hard, fine white stoneware body which can be stained with various iron oxides to give different colours. (Blue and green are the most common, but look out for yellow, lilac, white, black and even red.) **Use:** Mainly decorative wares. Later for decorative useful wares, such as teapots. Cups and saucers are rare. **Date of production:** *c.*1775 to the present day by Wedgwood. Other factories *c.*1800–1820 and again *c.*1900. **Where produced:** England. Some European factories made wares with the appearance of jasper, but made of biscuit porcelain.

Jasper was also developed by Wedgwood and is the ware most synonymous with the name today. Other factories, such as William Adams & Sons, produced similar wares in the late-19th century, but Wedgwood has been the most enduring.

Jasper takes two forms: 'solid' jasper where the body is stained right through with colour; and more common 'jasper dip', where only the surface is coloured. Decoration can be engine-turned but typically takes the form of applied white or coloured reliefs. Rarely a third colour is used and such three-colour pieces are very collectable. Large amounts of dark blue jasper ware were made in the late-19th century and large amounts of light blue jasper are made by Wedgwood today. These pieces are of much less value than similar, but usually more finely made, earlier pieces.

Caneware

Type: Fine fawn-coloured stoneware. Dry-bodied, non-porous. **Use:** Useful wares.
Date of production: *c.*1770s–1820.
Where produced: Staffordshire, England.

Also known as drabware, these types of wares are similar in appearance to jasper ware, but are always dull beige or occasionally a dull olive green. When unglazed, they have a matt velvety surface, but are also found lead-glazed. Decoration is usually engine-turned. Glazed pieces are sometimes embellished with gilding or with black transfer or bat printed decoration. Caneware is always neatly potted.

Caneware sugar bowl, c.1800

Red ware

Type: Fine red stoneware. Dry-bodied, non-porous. **Use:** Useful wares, smaller decorative items. **Date of production:** *c.*1690–1820. Revived by Wedgwood in the late 19th century under the name 'rosso antico'. **Where produced:** Staffordshire *c.*1690–1820. Meissen in the early 18th century and later. China.

Also known in England as 'rosso antico', red wares derive from a fine Chinese red stoneware from the province of Yixing. These wares were imported from China in the mid-17th century when tea drinking became fashionable. The first red wares made in imitation of these were produced in London, and later in Staffordshire from the 1680s onwards by the Elers brothers who had come to England from Holland. Other Staffordshire factories soon began to make red wares, Wedgwood calling his version 'rosso antico'. Red stoneware was developed by Böttger at Meissen *c.*1705, but was soon succeeded by his new porcelain body.

Decoration was simple, initially the shapes were moulded and later turned, and sprigged or applied with flowers or figures. Later items were engine-turned or painted.

Elers red ware teapot, c.1690

Yellow ware

A creamware or pearlware-type body covered in a yellow glaze, often a bright canary colour. Popular *c.*1800–1830. Decoration was usually transfer printed or painted.

Printed yellow ware, c.1810/20

Terracotta

A soft earthenware often used for brick making. Terracotta is also sometimes used for making large figures or groups, and by sculptors for maquettes or studies for large bronze or marble compositions. It is usually red in colour, but can also be a pale creamy-grey colour. The Goldscheider factory in Austria made large pale terracotta sculptural figures and plaques, often cold painted to simulate bronze.

Lilac porcelain

Lilac porcelain wares appeared in the early part of the 19th century and were popular with potters in the 1820s and '30s. Some small decorative miniature wares were made of lilac-tinted porcelain, and it was popular with the makers of pastille burners, notably the highly collectable cottage shapes.

Lilac porcelain sprigged mug, c.1840

TYPES OF DECORATION

Introduction

While the previous chapter has looked at the different types of wares made by ceramic manufacturers, this chapter will try to illustrate some of the types of decoration used on these wares. Identifying the nature of the decoration on an object can give clues to its age and country of origin. Decoration can take many forms: it can be printed, painted, applied in relief or moulded. It can be overglaze, underglaze or even the glaze itself. This section will also look at lustre decoration and gilding, explaining some of the technical detail as simply as possible.

Different decorative techniques developed as potters strove to emulate not only imports from the East but also their own local competitors. Potters were not only competing with one another, but also with silversmiths and sculptors, particularly in the making of more decorative items; as a result, they began to imitate marble, hard stones, ormolu and silver.

Royal Crown Derby vase, richly decorated in a variety of techniques, c.1890/1900 ▶

Painted underglaze and tin-glaze decoration

The following are examples of decoration where colour is painted either on to the biscuit ware before glaze is added, or to the opaque tin glaze before it is fired. In each case the colour fuses into the glaze, and is therefore not subject to surface wear or deterioration.

COBALT BLUE

Cobalt is the substance from which most blue colours on pottery and porcelain are derived and its popularity in Europe stems from the large quantities of underglaze blue-decorated porcelains imported from China and Japan. On porcelain and some earthenwares the blue colour is painted on to biscuit ware before being covered in a lead glaze. The resulting colour can vary from a grey blue-black to a bright clear royal blue, depending on the impurities in the cobalt. This is described as

Caughley 'trial' mug, c.1770, showing colour tests

underglaze-blue. Where not covered by glaze, the cobalt fires as black. On tin-glazed wares the cobalt is painted on to the surface of the white glaze and when fired melts and fuses with the glaze. Cobalt was also used to stain clay blue for use in marbled wares.

Other colours

RED

This colour often appears either as underglaze in combination with blue on porcelains, or tin-glazed wares. Red is usually created from an oxide of iron or copper.

MANGANESE

Powdered manganese was sprinkled onto tin glazes to give a mottled purple ground colour, known as powdered manganese. Manganese mixed with a lead glaze gives the distinctive brown and purple glaze colours of 'Whieldon-type' ware.

Caughley mug, dated 1779

Colours such as green, ochre, black and yellow also appear under or in the glaze.

Other types of glazed ware

PRATTWARE

The term Prattware is used to describe a type of ware made in Staffordshire *c.*1780–1840, which used a distinctive underglaze colour palette of green, brown, ochre, yellow and blue. Supposedly first used by William Pratt (hence the name), numerous factories made wares of this type, usually with a pearlware body.

MOCHA WARE

Mocha is a distinctive type of inexpensive utilitarian earthware such as mugs and jugs decorated with bands of colour and attractive tree-like designs. The decoration occurs when a liquid alkaline oxide colour is added to a slightly acidic slip surface. The two substances react causing the colour to spread rapidly and at random away from the point of contact. The resulting effect is often like a brown tree with many leafy branches. This ware was most popular during the first half of the 19th century, although mocha decoration was first introduced in the late 18th century and continued into this century. Several small and a few larger Staffordshire companies produced this wear which was also manufactured in Tyne and Wear, South Wales, Bristol, Derbyshire and Glasgow.

BIANCO-SOPRA-BIANCO

This type of decoration was used on mostly English Delftware and consisted of white enamel painted on to a blue-tinted tin glaze, fired to give a slightly relief white on blue surface decoration.

Prattware tea canister, c.1800, moulded and typically coloured

Surface painted decoration

ENAMEL COLOURS

The idea of painting with coloured enamels on to the glazed surface of ware first appeared in the 17th century and was probably inspired by potters looking at painted enamels on Venetian glassware. Although appearing first on 17th-century pottery, enamel colours were soon used on porcelain as well, being fired on to the glaze in a second firing. On soft paste porcelain the colours tend to sink into the glaze and on hard paste they tend to stay on the surface. As this is a surface decoration fired at relatively low temperatures, enamel paint is prone to wear and, in time, if the ware is used heavily, the

Chelsea dish, c.1755, with enamel painted decoration

decoration can eventually wear away, leaving only a ghostly shadow of the pattern on the surface.

It is worth remembering when looking at a complex enamel painted scene that the colours change in the firing, and that part of the artist's skill is in selecting the colours and knowing what the final fired result will be.

MONOCHROME

Painting a subject entirely in one colour became popular in the 18th century and continued into the early 19th century. This technique was also known as painting *en grisaille* when black was used or *en camaieu* when painting in several tones of the same colour. Painting in one colour allowed an artist to concentrate on composition rather than colour, like a drawing.

ENCAUSTIC DECORATION

Encaustic or burnt on decoration was used by Wedgwood for the painted decoration of his black basalt and rosso antico wares. The resulting colours tend to be rather dry and matt, the technique presumably attempting to emulate the matt appearance of Greek and Roman pottery.

Group of black basalt wares, some with gilt and encaustic decoration

Printed decoration

First developed in England, printing was soon found to be a relatively cheap method of decorating an item with a complex pattern which would have been extremely time consuming (and costly) to paint by hand. There are several different types of printing methods but the earliest was transfer printing.

TRANSFER PRINTING

This involves engraving a pattern on to a metal plate which is then inked with colour. A special paper is then pressed on to the metal plate, picking up the colour; then the paper is pressed on to the object to be decorated, 'transferring' the design to the surface of the ware. The object is then fired and the paper burns away, leaving the design intact. The earliest engravers producing designs for printing on porcelain and Delft were Robert Hancock at Worcester, and John Sadler and Guy Green at Liverpool, all in the 1750s. These engravers either invented new subjects or adapted popular prints. Colours used initially were black, blue, purple and red.

By the late 18th century, blue had become the predominant colour used for printing on pearlwares. So-called 'blue and white' transfer printing became the preferred decoration for dinner services in the early 19th century and remains popular to the present day. The perennially popular 'willow pattern' is a good example.

Worcester transfer printed mug, c.1770

Other forms of printing

BAT PRINTING

Bats were soft, flexible glue sheets used in the late 18th and early 19th centuries as an alternative to paper. An impression from a metal engraving was taken in oil, transferred to the ware and then dusted with powdered colour. Black was the main colour used, with red-brown used occasionally; there are also rare examples produced in gold. Bat prints were stipple engraved rather than line engraved. Black prints tend to appear grey and the subjects are often small and very detailed. The Spode factory was one of the major producers of bat printed porcelains in the early 19th century.

COLOUR PRINTING

The previous two methods are almost always limited to just one colour, occasionally two. Multiple-colour printing is attributed to the engraver Jesse Austin in the 1840s and its production is associated with the Staffordshire firm of F. & R. Pratt of Fenton. This process used several engraved copper plates to produce

Bat-printed tea cup and saucer, c.1810

a multi-coloured image. The basic colours used were red, yellow, blue and a final over-print in black to give definition. This technique was used mainly on pot lids which are now very collectable *(see page 208)*, but was also used to decorate some useful wares.

This technique was clearly difficult and time-consuming and was gradually replaced by litho printing at the turn of the century. This process employed the use of factory-produced pre-inked sheets of virtually any design. In the early part of the century it was popular for potters to use litho print designs which appeared to be hand painted and it is sometimes difficult to tell the difference between some of the printed and painted patterns. Litho printing also became popular elsewhere in Europe, where up to this point ceramics patterns had remained mainly hand painted.

Detail of illustration on page 60

Hand painted or printed?

It is useful to be able to tell the difference between hand painted and printed wares, partly in order to date and identify the piece, and partly because of the effect it can have on the value of a piece, as hand painted wares are often (sometimes wrongly) perceived as being of greater intrinsic quality and hence of more value. The following details show close-ups of printed and painted decoration, and the list of points shows what to look out for:

- Later colour prints are made up of tiny dots like a large poster.
- Painted wares have a smooth brushstroke of solid colour.

Detail of hand painting

- Prints are flat and therefore when applied to a curved surface inevitably fold and overlap. These folds are particularly noticeable on cheaper wares.
- Prints often have to be cut to size; as a result, joins and tears are often noticeable.
- Designs can be smudged if the paper transfer slips.
- A painted design is made to fit the available area and should never appear to run out of space as a print might.
- If you have two pieces with the same pattern, compare the two. There will be small variations in painted patterns but not in printed ones.
- Be aware of patterns which are printed but have painted edges or painted white highlights. Many Continental factories tried hard to make their decoration appear hand painted in this way.
- Many English factories in the 19th century used a printed outline filled in with colour.

Detail of printed decoration

Lustre

Lustre decoration is aptly summed up by W. B. Honey as 'a film of metal reduced from an oxide or sulphide, produced on the surface of an item either as a complete covering or painted design'.

Essentially lustre is iridescent or metallic painted decoration and is applied after a piece has been glazed. The item is then refired in a kiln with smoke-producing materials. The carbon from the smoke unites with the oxygen in the pigment leaving a layer of metal on the ware. The technique sounds relatively simple but it was all but lost for several hundred years, and even when attempted by experienced potters many pieces misfired, due to incorrect kiln conditions. Early lustre wares were produced in Spain from the 12th century onwards and are known as 'hispano moresque' wares.

Hispano-moresque vase, early 18th century

Lustre decoration was used in small amounts by Böttger at Meissen in the 1730s. In Staffordshire, a different technique, using platinum salts, gave a silver effect and gold was used to make purple or copper lustre.

Only one colour was used at a time and decoration was simple, using waxed areas to 'resist' the lustre and so create a pattern.

The reducing technique was brought to England by William de Morgan in the 19th century. He had worked in Italy, learning the art of lustre decoration at factories there, and was able to produce high quality complex designs. Lustre decoration was also used by Pilkingtons Royal Lancastrian factory and by Royal Doulton, where simulated silver and copper wares were made in the early part of this century.

Sunderland lustre jug, c.1820

Gilding

Gilding is usually found on porcelain and some fine earthenwares, although the Dutch briefly produced 'Delft doree' (tin-glazed earthenware with gilding added) in an attempt to compete with porcelain products.

Although a type of lustre decoration, gilding deserves to be looked at separately. The addition of gilding to an item has traditionally been seen as adding a final touch of quality or class. Today this is not necessarily the case as adding a gilt rim to a piece can be done relatively easily. In the past, however, gilding was time-consuming and costly, and the more gilding on a piece, the higher the price. There were various methods of gilding, all of which involved the use of real gold, as is the case today.

Parcel gilding is the solid gilding of entire sections of a piece, popular in France in the Empire period. Often this was done in an attempt to emulate gilt bronze (ormolu) or silver gilt wares. Gilding is sometimes heightened by the addition of **jewelling.** This is the use of translucent dots of enamel on gold foil to simulate precious stones. On early Meissen wares precious stones were in fact laid into wares. Jewelling was also used at the Sèvres factory and at Coalport in England.

Gilding can also be **tooled** or carved with acid to create texture and patterns on an otherwise flat surface. Some areas are left matt, others burnished to heighten the effect. Tooled gilt borders were particularly popular on dinner and dessert services at the turn of this century and could be very costly.

Flight Barr and Barr pot pourri jar, c.1820, showing gilding

Textured and coloured clay decoration

The following are some of the techniques of decoration involving the removal or addition to the body of clay or slip.

INLAID AND INCISED DECORATION

- **Sgraffito:** Decoration made by scratching or incising the design through the applied slip to reveal the body beneath.
- **Incised:** Design scratched directly into the clay body.
- **Inlay:** Insertion of a design in one coloured clay into a surface of a different colour (used frequently for tiles).

RELIEF DECORATION

- **Moulding:** Pressing the body of a piece into a mould to create shape before firing.
- **Casting:** Pouring liquid slip into a mould to cast a shape.
- **Tube-lining:** Piping slip on to a surface to give a raised outline, sometimes to create a pattern as with early slipwares; alternatively used to form an outline to be filled with coloured glazes, a technique used by the Moorcroft pottery.
- **Impressed:** Stamping metal dies into the soft unfired surface.

Moorcroft vase, 1930s

- **Applied relief:** Making low relief shapes in moulds and applying them to the surface.
- **Encrusting:** Hand-made shapes (often flowers), applied to the surface. So-called 'schneeballen' wares are encrusted with small flowerheads.

PIERCED DECORATION

Also known as **reticulated,** pierced decoration can vary from simple holes punched into a rim, through open basketweave borders, to the complex entirely reticulated wares produced by George Owen at Royal Worcester in the early part of this century.

Royal Worcester reticulated vase, c.1910

SURFACE SLIP DECORATION

Coloured clays were sometimes mixed to create a marbled body referred to as 'solid agate'. This same effect was also achieved by applying a marbled slip of various coloured clays onto a single-coloured ware. Wedgwood used this technique to simulate porphyry and other marble stones. Marble effects were also created by the Staffordshire potters on creamware by the use of mottled coloured glazes; these are known as 'Whieldon-type' wares.

Monochrome and flambé glazes

Surface decoration is not always painted, printed or applied. Wares may rely on glaze alone for decorative effect, and have done so since the earliest Chinese porcelains. Glazes are often clear to reveal the decoration or colour of body beneath, but this is not always the case.

The Chinese created a mottled red glaze known as *sang de boeuf* and a pale green glaze known as *celadon.* European potters were inspired by Chinese wares and tried to emulate these glazes, often with mixed results. Notable makers of coloured glazed wares include the Ruskin pottery in England during the early part of this century, Pilkingtons, Sèvres and Royal Doulton. William Howson Taylor at Ruskin became particularly adept at producing technically difficult, high-fired red and purple flambé glazes. Royal Doulton had ranges called 'Flambé', 'Sung' and 'Chang', the latter two named after their Oriental inspiration.

More recently, studio potters have tended to concentrate on glazed effects for decoration, with glaze complimenting the shape and form, allowing function to take precedence over surface decoration.

Ruskin flambé vase and stand, c.1910

FORM AND FUNCTION

Introduction

This chapter deals with the different shapes of ceramic wares which are usually divided into 'useful' and 'useless'. Useful wares are generally functional items such as dinner, tea and dessert wares; useless wares are more decorative items such as vases and figures. The dividing lines are not so clear cut, as a simple vase can be eminently functional, whereas a flower-encrusted teapot is not at all practical.

The following pages outline some of the shapes which can be found, and suggest how looking at shapes can help with dating and identification. Potters were extremely imaginative and were constantly striving to produce better, more modern versions of their standard objects. They still

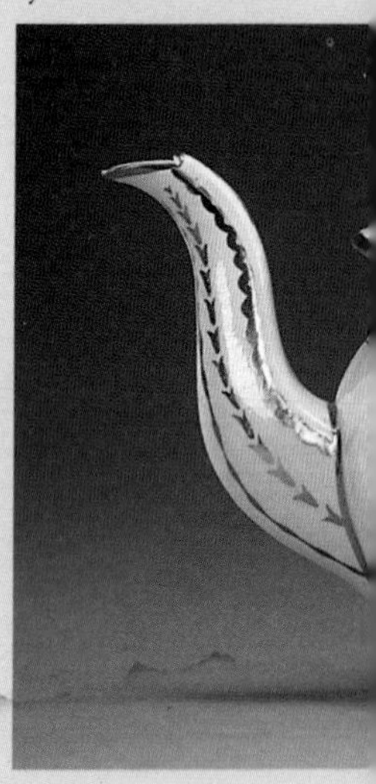

Staffordshire English teapot, c.1810/20

are. But first, it is useful to examine the way ceramic wares are actually produced and to look at some of the problems potters have had to overcome in order to be able to create bigger objects and more complex shapes.

Having read this section in combination with the previous two it should be possible for someone attempting to identify a ceramic object to at least narrow down the options with regard to date and place of origin and so know in which direction to go in order to finally identify the piece.

Methods of production

The following diagram shows simply the stages involved in producing a ceramic object.

Preparing the body

Mix water, clay and other ingredients, (bone, for example)

↓

Plastic clay made into shape

or

Liquid clay (slip) poured into mould

↓

Drying

Applied or incised decoration is carried out at this stage

↓

Biscuit firing

↓

Underglaze colour applied

↓

Glaze applied – dipped or sprayed

↓

Glost (second) firing to fix glaze

↓

Decoration (enamel) applied

Fired again

↓

Gilding

↓

Burnishing

Separate chapters have looked at the different types of body and decoration, but have not explained the various methods of actually making an object. The three basic methods are:

- **Handbuilding:** Pinching, coiling and slab building.
- **Moulding:** Press moulding and casting.
- **Throwing:** Using a wheel.

All three methods were used up to the 19th century. With the advent of industrialization, slip casting became the most common factory method of production, although handbuilding and throwing methods continued to be used by some 19th-century art potters and by studio potters in this century. Complex objects such as figures were, and still are, made in different sections and the component parts were assembled by workers known as 'repairers'. To get a better idea of the complexity of making even a small ceramic object, it would be useful to visit one of the many ceramic factories which are open to the public, where each stage and method of production is explained in detail.

Throwing a vase

Kiln furniture

When an object goes into the kiln for its first firing, the clay is still relatively soft and can warp or alter in shape if not supported properly. This support is provided by a series of ceramic or metal objects, known as kiln furniture, which have been designed to prevent the different shaped objects from collapsing during the firing. Plates were stacked on top of one another with stilts between them, leaving small marks on the back of each plate.

It must be remembered that heating a kiln to the temperature required to fire the clay is costly and as a result, as many pieces as possible must be fitted into a kiln for firing.

Because making some items was so complicated and time consuming, it was not only perfect items which were subsequently sold. Most factories have traditionally sold 'seconds' – pieces with minor imperfections. Badly damaged items were known as 'wasters' or 'shards' and were dumped.The excavation of such dumps can supply today's researchers with information about what type of wares a factory was producing. This is particularly applicable to some of the early English porcelain factories for which no written records exist.

Shapes

Services

Many ceramic objects for sale today as individual pieces or small groups started life as part of a service. Individual shapes will be described in later sections, but the following pages give an idea of what types of services existed and their shapes.

Dinner services have been made in pottery and porcelain since the early 18th century, forming a less expensive and more functional decorative alternative to silver. Early shapes were heavily influenced by silver and the range of wares included in a dinner service was large.

English ironstone dinner service, c.1820

• Services would include large tureens for soup, usually with covers, stands and ladles. Smaller tureens for sauces often have a distinct foot, occasionally with an attached stand. Sauce boats were an alternative to tureens. They were of similar form to modern sauce boats, although variations included double-lipped boats with two handles and sometimes an integral fixed stand.

• Meat serving dishes, usually in graduated sizes, dinner plates, soup plates and cheese plates would form the so-called 'flatwares'. Side plates for bread and kidney-shaped dishes for salad were a 19th-century addition.

• Covered dishes were usually included for vegetables and long oval dishes were used for serving fish.

• Additional items could include small open dishes used for serving salt and pickles.

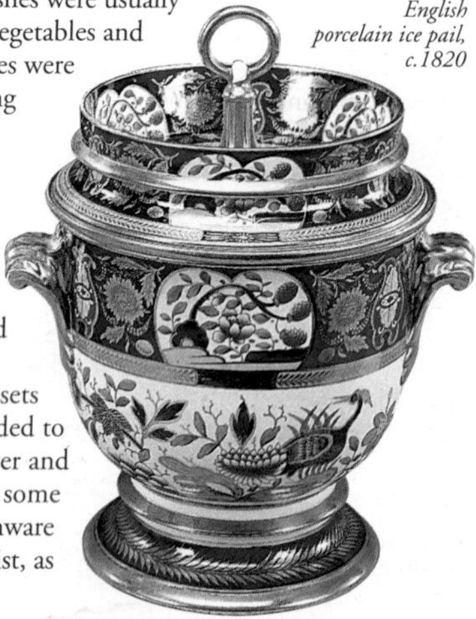

English porcelain ice pail, c.1820

Condiment sets and stands tended to be made in silver and glass; although some elaborate creamware examples do exist, as do individual condiment bottles and pots, they are relatively rare.

- Egg cups are also a rarity until the mid-19th century, although examples do exist.

Many dinner services were huge and comprised hundreds of pieces. Serving dishes of all forms command a premium when they appear for sale, as they are always much rarer than the corresponding plates which would have been made in far larger numbers.

Dessert services appeared in the mid-18th century. They were used to serve fruit, nuts or sweetmeats after a meal, and their decoration is often more elaborate than dinner services as they were less frequently used. Traditionally they also tended to be made of porcelain, while dinner services were often of earthenware or ironstone.

- Many 18th- and 19th-century services comprised numerous shaped shallow serving bowls and perhaps one centre basket, along with plates of slightly smaller size than those used for dinner.
- The more elaborate services also have tureens for sauce, as well as large pails with covers and liners designed to be filled with crushed ice and fruit.

Dessert services remained popular into the late 19th century, when almost every middle-class household had a separate dessert service of some sort. These later services are invariably made of porcelain and tended to comprise two tall-footed stands, four or six low stands and twelve or eighteen plates. The factories around Limoges in France were particularly prolific in the production of such services, of which numerous examples survive today.

Tea and coffee services became popular when it became fashionable to drink these beverages in the early 18th century, and early services follow silver or Chinese porcelain shapes. Sets included a teapot with cover and stand, cream or milk jug, sometimes a hot water jug, sugar bowl or sugar box, usually with a cover, slop bowl and either teabowls or tea cups, coffee cups or cans. Early saucers were large and quite deep, and one saucer served both tea and coffee cups. Extras often included matching spoon tray and tea canister. By the middle of the 19th century, tea and coffee services began to include side plates and one saucer for each cup, and sugar bowls had become open.

By the Edwardian period in Britain, no household was complete without a 'best china' tea service and a corresponding coffee set. Since these services were considered for best use only they tended to be little used, so survive in quite large numbers, and are often of disappointingly low value today.

English teawares, c.1810

In the late 19th century, sets often came without teapots, presumably intending the use of a silver one, and tea and coffee sets began to be sold separately.

Dinner, dessert and tea and coffeee services were the three main services in general use. Other sets or services included so-called **cabaret sets** for tea, coffee or chocolate, with the main serving pieces designed to stand on a tray with one or two cups and saucers. A variation on this theme is the 19th-century 'lazy Susan' – a revolving tray designed to stand in the centre of the table and often fitted with a central tea urn and with matching cups and saucers. Alternatively, the tray could be fitted with shaped segmented dishes and covers, around a central bowl. These are known as **supper sets.** Supper sets were particularly popular in the late 18th and early 19th centuries, and creamware and blue printed pieces can often be found for sale at shops and fairs. Complete sets are extremely rare.

Berlin cabaret service, c.1880

Teapots

The habit of tea drinking came to Europe from China in the mid-17th century and with it came teapots of red Yixing stoneware. These pots were soon copied in England and Europe and early shapes were globular with simple loop handles and short straight spouts. The idea of coffee drinking came via Turkey at a similar date and the generally taller coffee pot shapes reflect the shape of Turkish vessels of this early period. Coffee pots have mostly retained this basic shape, the tall baluster form being popular even today. The shape of teapots has altered many times, and shape can be a helpful guide to date, although later copies can confuse matters! The subject of teapots and the development of their shapes is covered in a number of specialist books and lack of illustration space means that a detailed discussion can not be made here. The following is a brief guide to shape and date:

- **Late 17th–early 18th century** Globular shapes as described above.
- **1740–50** Bullet-shaped pots.
- **Mid 18th-century** Novelty pots popular. Sometimes found in the shape of vegetables or figures.
- ***c.*1770** Globular and cylindrical pots in creamware, the former often raised on 'paw' feet.

Meissen bullet-shaped teapot, c.1735

• **c.1800** Commode shapes. 'Cadogan' pots also appear at this date. These are filled from underneath and have no cover. Usually brown-glazed with gilt detail, these were made throughout the 19th century by various makers.
• **c.1812–20s** 'London' shape popular in England.
• **c.1830–50** Round and rococo shapes popular. Teapots became taller, with scroll moulding and elaborate handles.
• **c.1850–1900** Novelty teapots again popular. Minton made several amusing majolica pots in this period.
• **Late 19th century** Patent 'self-pouring' teapots appear. Doulton made such a pot with a central sleeve which could be raised, causing tea to pour from the spout.
• **1920s–30s** Art Deco shapes. Triangular handles appear. Sadler in Staffordshire produced novelty pots in the shape of racing cars and aeroplanes.

Teapots were expensive objects in the 18th century. They were often given as presents and are sometimes found inscribed with dates and verse. They were also prone to cracking from the hot water. Delftware was particularly unsuited to tea- and coffee-making so tea wares are virtually unknown in Delft. Today teapots are collected for the variety of shapes produced and prized because of their relative rarity compared with contemporary cups and saucers.

Staffordshire rococo teapot, c.1840

Cups

Although originally made as parts of services, cups are collected in their own right, either as teacup and saucer sets, coffee cups on their own or as trios of teacup, coffee cup and shared saucer.

The first teacups took the form of small deep bowls, after Chinese originals. Known as teabowls, they continued to be popular until *c.*1800, but from the mid-18th century teacups were also made, usually of slightly broader shape than the teabowls and with a loop handle. Coffee cups that appeared during this time were traditionally taller and narrower than teacups and this convention continues today. Straight-sided coffee cans

Collection of English coffee cups, c.1750/60

appeared in the late 18th century and were popular until the 1830s, being revived again this century, notably by Susie Cooper at Wedgwood in the 1960s. In the second quarter of the 19th century, teacups were made extremely broad and shallow and decoration was put inside. Unfortunately, this means that these pieces are often badly worn inside.

Variations of tea and coffee cups include **giant cups** made in Staffordshire in the second half of the 19th century, **chocolate cups** with two handles and a cover, and **trembleuse cups** that fit into an indented stand, or have a pierced frame into which they fit added to the saucer. Not all cups were intended for use, and in the late 18th and 19th centuries, various factories produced **cabinet cups,** intended for display only. These are usually highly decorated and many have impractical gilt interiors.

Traditional cup forms are popular today, although potters have tried to create variation. In the 1930s the Shelley potteries produced conical cups with solid triangular handles, but these were disliked and condemned as inelegant. The factory bowed to pressure and pierced the triangle, making the handle more like the traditional loop.

Shelley 'Mode' shape, c.1930/31

Mugs and loving cups

Mugs in various forms date back to the 18th century when they were usually used to hold alcoholic beverages. Continental vessels were usually straight sided, or baluster form, and often had a hinged pewter or gilt-metal cover to protect the contents. English mugs were more likely to be open at the top, occasionally with a metal mounted rim. In this century the use of mugs for drinking ale has declined in favour of the glass, but the mug, in slightly smaller form, has had a renaissance as a vessel for tea and coffee drinking. These modern mugs are now beginning to be collected in their own right.

The following describes some of the various guises mugs can take:

- **Tankard:** Usually a name ascribed to early vessels with lids.
- **Loving cups:** A mug with two handles, allegedly for lovers to hold one handle each. These vessels are often large and decorative, with presentation inscriptions or drinking mottoes.
- **Tyg:** A type of large drinking mug, usually with two or four handles, but it may have up to eleven handles arranged equidistantly around the exterior. Essentially decorative vessels.
- **Frog mug:** A mug or loving cup into the bottom of which the potter adds a pottery frog. The intention is to shock the drinker as it is revealed when he has drunk most of the contents. The most ingenious of these are made so that the last dregs of liquid actually seem to

flow from the open mouth of the frog. These mugs date back to the late 18th century but there are many poor-quality, late 19th-century examples and even modern reproductions.

Nuremberg tankard, c.1760

Jugs

Jugs were made in a variety of shapes and sizes, and are commonly collected. Jugs for milk or cream were originally made as parts of tea services and their form often follows that of the teapot. Some 18th-century cream jugs were made with covers but to find them still intact is rare. A popular form of cream jug with the English factories from the 1750s until about 1790, was the so-called 'sparrow beak' cream jug. This is a squat baluster-shaped jug with a distinctive triangular spout (like the beak of a sparrow). Some examples can still be found with covers. Other notable types of jugs include:

- **Large water jugs:** Formed part of 19th- and 20th-century toilet sets.
- **Decorative jugs:** These jugs for wine and water were made from relief-moulded stoneware in the mid-19th century.
- **Giant milk and wine jugs:** Made in Staffordshire in the 19th century with an extra handle beneath the spout to aid pouring.
- **Novelty jugs:** An example of this is the jug designed by Mabel Lucie Attwell in the form of a saluting pixie for the Shelley potteries.
- **Puzzle jugs:** These

Sparrow-beak cream jug, c.1770

were made as tavern novelties to fool unsuspecting drinkers. They would have pierced necks and multiple spouts, the trick being to empty the jug by a combination of tilting the jug, sucking and blocking the correct spouts, without getting soaked by the contents.

- **Graduated sets of three or five jugs:** These were common in Staffordshire *c.*1900, and numerous sets survive today, generally of poor quality.

Pearlware puzzle jug, c.1820

Bowls

Bowls tend to be far less collected than the previous shapes of ware discussed, mainly because they are difficult to display. Exterior decoration can only be seen if the object is above eye level, while interior decoration is often hidden by the contents and is prone to wear. One result of the above is that bowls are relatively cheap to buy and even interesting 18th-century examples can be bought for as little as £50. The following are a few of the types of bowls made by potters since the early 18th century:

- **Sugar bowls:** Early ones have covers and are known as *sucriers* or sugar boxes.
- **Slop bowls:** Often mistaken for sugar bowls, slop bowls were an essential part of all pre-1850 tea services and were intended for cold tea slops. They were much larger than modern sugar bowls, usually 12–15cm (5–6in) across.
- **Wash bowls:** These formed part of the bedroom toilet set. Often mistaken for punch bowls, they differ by having a turned over rim which enabled them to be easily carried, essential when full of water!
- **Punch bowls:** Usually slightly deeper than toilet bowls, these were popular *c.*1800 and usually have a low foot and fairly straight sides.
- **Barbers' bowls:** These have a semi-

circular piece cut out of the rim to enable the bowl to be pushed up to the neck of the person being shaved. They fell from use after the mid-19th century.

- **Bleeding bowls:** Similar in shape to barbers' bowls but deeper and without the cutaway rim. They were used by doctors when bleeding a patient.
- **Monteiths:** A deep bowl with an undulating rim, a monteith was filled with iced water and wine glasses were suspended from the rim by their feet, their bowls resting in the chilled water. The shape derives from silver.

Wedgwood fairyland lustre punch bowl, 1920s

Plates

The various sizes of plates which originally formed parts of dinner or dessert services have already been mentioned, but plates have not always been made for purely functional purposes. The plates which command the highest prices tend to be those made as single items for display rather than for use.

- **Chargers:** These large plates were intended to sit flat in the centre of a table or hang on a wall. Many Delftware and Italian maiolica chargers were intended for display rather than use, the large flat expanse forming an ideal canvas for the ceramic artist.
- **Cabinet plates:** As the name suggests, these are intended for display. They tend to be of dinner plate size or slightly smaller, and were popular in the late 18th and early 19th centuries. Notable makers of cabinet plates were the factories at Vienna, Sèvres and Berlin. A typical Continental cabinet plate will have a painted centre within rich gilt borders. English factories made cabinet plates throughout the 19th century with Coalport, Minton and the Worcester factories producing some very elaborate examples.
- **Plate warmers:** Included in large dinner services, these appear to be ordinary plates on the surface but have an enclosed well underneath designed to be filled with hot water. Dinner plates were then stacked on top of the plate warmer to remove the chill without danger of damage from too intense a heat. Many plate warmers are erroneously described as food warmers which, although

of similar shape, only appeared in the latter 19th century, and were always made with matching covers.

- **Square plates:** These were occasionally made by potters, notably Clarice Cliff in the early 1930s. They are invariably unsuccessful as the shape has a tendency to warp during firing, and having four corners, are extremely prone to chipping during use.

Berlin cabinet plate, c.1814

Baskets

Baskets in pottery and porcelain were made as parts of dessert services or as single items to hold fruit, nuts or sweetmeats. Some factories, particularly Belleek in Ireland, specialized in open 'basketweave' baskets made from woven strands of clay. These are technically difficult to produce and are intended for display rather than use. Other baskets include:

- **Chestnut baskets:** Roast chestnuts were popularly enjoyed after dinner in the latter half of the 18th century, and baskets with pierced sides and loop handles were made especially to contain them.
- **Shallow oval or rectangular form:** Other popular shapes of baskets included ovals and rectangles with overhead loop handles. These were produced particularly by English makers in the period 1820–40, and are usually highly decorated, often with encrusted as well as painted decoration.
- **Basket table centrepieces:** These elaborate baskets were popular in the 19th century. Mostly from German factories in

Dresden and Thuringia, they are often pierced, painted or printed with flowers and encrusted with fruit and foliage, usually above a tall, sometimes figural, stem.

• **Miniatures:** Various shapes of basket were also copied in miniature, the shape presumably having more decorative appeal than many functional wares.

Worcester chestnut basket, c.1770

Other table and serving wares

The following is a list of other pottery and porcelain items used for eating and drinking which may not have been included as part of a service.

• **Cutlery:** Pottery and porcelain handles for knives and forks appeared in the mid-18th century, in porcelain at Meissen in Germany, and at various English porcelain factories, as well as in agate and 'Whieldon-type' wares. Early shapes followed silver, either with a simple 'pistol' handle, or a waisted shape with rococo scroll moulding. Few English factories made cutlery handles in the 19th century, although Continental makers continued to do so. There was a revival in England *c.*1900, with Royal Crown Derby producing sets of porcelain-handled fruit knives in popular patterns, and many Staffordshire factories produced sets of salad bowls with matching ceramic-handled silver-plated servers. Such sets are relatively common.

Other Wares Include:

• **Salts:** In the 18th century, salt was served in an open bowl rather than a pot.

• **Butter tubs:** These were often shaped to simulate a small wooden tub with flat cover.

• **Pickle dishes:** Traditionally leaf-shaped.

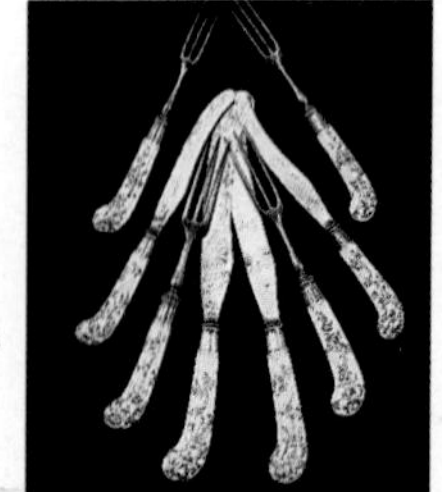

Bow cutlery handles, c.1758

Worcester pickle dish, c.1760

- **Jam or honey pots and covers:** These were sometimes in the form of beehives.
- **Biscuit barrels:** Very popular in the late 19th century, biscuit barrels are usually cylindrical or ovoid with silver or silver-plated covers.
- **Cheese dishes:** Large cheese domes designed to cover an entire Stilton appeared in the mid-19th century, followed by wedge-shaped dishes for a section of cheese. In the early part of this century, dishes became smaller and smaller, although retaining the classic wedge shape.

Other vessels designed for drink rather than food include:

- **Beakers:** Simple mugs without handles were used in bedrooms for water during the 19th century.
- **Spirit barrels:** Pottery spirit barrels were made throughout the 19th century. Some large brown stoneware examples were purely functional, while other more decorative smaller examples stood in bars and were used for dispensing drinks. Frequently these are inscribed with the name of the brewer. Porcelain examples are rare, although faience dispensers for wine do exist.

Brown stoneware spirit flask, 19th century

Vases

The idea of using ceramic vases for decoration came to Europe from China in the 17th century. Sets of vases intended to decorate chimney breasts became known as *garniture de cheminée* and usually comprised a pair of trumpet-shaped vases and three vases with covers, often of baluster form. These Chinese blue and white decorated sets were widely imitated in Dutch Delft and later in porcelain. They were not intended to hold flowers but were purely decorative.

Some of the earliest flower vases proper, were Dutch Delft **tulip vases** in which tulips were grown. These were usually tall pyramid-like constructions comprising several separate tiers, and are extremely rare today. Smaller bulb or tulip vases are more common, and again, are usually found in Delft.

Around the turn of the 18th century **bough pots** became fashionable. These were intended to hold small branches rather than flowers and were often of D-shaped sections with detachable covers pierced with holes to hold the branches in place.

Davenport bough pot, c.1810

They were particularly popular in England, and fine examples were made at Derby and Worcester.

These two factories were, along with most others, active in producing **spill vases.** These were short vases, often of cylindrical form, intended to sit on a mantelpiece and hold spills, wax tapers used for lighting fires. They were originally made in pairs, but frequently only single examples survive.

Another form of vase which should also be mentioned is the **cornucopia vase** or wall pocket, designed to hang flat on a wall. These were produced in porcelain in the 18th century, with the traditional cornucopia shape giving way to more unusual forms, including face masks. Wall pocket vases had a renaissance in the late 19th century with Continental makers such as Sitzendorf producing examples heavily encrusted with flowers and cherubs. Wall masks and mask pockets were revived in the 1920s–30s by Art Deco designers. As the 19th century wore on, vase forms became more elaborate and diverse, with vases beginning to be used to hold flowers. During this century vases have become simpler in style and with some studio potters, they have evolved from functional vessels into sculptural forms, entirely unsuited to practical purposes.

Royal Worcester vase, c.1910/20

Ornamental wares

The previous pages have looked principally at useful items, where function has tended to dictate form. The following items are all commonly found in pottery and porcelain, and have a useful purpose, but one which often does not influence external shape.

Clock cases: Porcelain panels set into the metal cases of clocks were a popular form of decoration in the 18th century. Cases made entirely of porcelain began to appear in the 19th century and examples from the second half of the century are quite commonly found. The movements were often of poor or standard mass-produced quality, the main purpose of the clock being for decorative effect. Notable makers included Meissen in Germany and Jacob Petit in France. In England in the early part of this century, potters produced cheaply made clock garnitures comprising a clock and two vases to stand on either side. These often have transfer printed decoration and are of little value.

Watch stands: These were popular in the late 18th and first half of the 19th centuries and were designed to hold a pocket watch when it was not being worn, so as to display the face. Prattware examples can be found in the form of a grandfather-style clock flanked by two figures, designed so that the watch rests in a pocket behind the top of the clock, forming its face.

Pastille burners: Pastilles were sweetly scented tablets used in the first half of the 19th century to scent a room. They were lit and gave off scented smoke. Burners

Meissen clock case, 19th century

were usually made of porcelain and sometimes had a lower section into which ash could drop. Many novelty burners were made, often in the form of cottages and castles, with chimneys and windows pierced to allow the smoke to slowly emerge. Such pieces can be distinguished from ordinary models of buildings by an arched opening in the back which allowed the pastille to be put in and the remains removed.

Pot pourri vases and bowls: The use of pot pourri was the alternative method of scenting a room, and examples of holders for these scented petals date back to the 18th century. Vases usually have pierced outer covers and a solid inner cover, which could be used to retain the fresh smell of the petals when the room was unoccupied, and removed to allow a much stronger smell to escape when required. Unlike pastilles, the use

Coalbrookdale inkstand, c.1835

of pot pourri continued to be popular throughout the 19th century. The Royal Worcester factory in England seems almost to have specialized in pot pourri vases and a large number exist today with extremely fine quality painted and gilt decoration.

Desk wares: As both are non-porous when glazed, pottery and porcelain were used to make inkwells and other desk wares. The shapes often followed traditional metalwork examples, but there were exceptions, particularly the heavily flower-encrusted wares made at Coalport and Coalbrookdale in the 1820s–30s. Unfortunately ceramic was not as good a medium for containing ink and many desk wares are badly stained where ink has penetrated the body through craze lines in the glaze. Desk wares are very collectable, and prices for complete sets in good condition are often high.

Gallanteriën

Gallanterien is a German word which is a blanket term for small decorative items such as boxes, scent bottles and thimbles of 18th-century origin. These types of wares are sometimes described in English as 'toys' and the most prolific maker of such pieces in England was the Chelsea factory during the 1750s–60s.

Scent bottles, small seals and snuff boxes were produced in quite large numbers at Chelsea and were often moulded in the shapes of figures, animals or fruit. Similarly, Meissen and other German factories produced snuff boxes, thimbles and *etuis,* small cases fitted with sewing implements. Most small boxes were intended for snuff, and usually had gold or silver mounts and hinges to enable the cover to be airtight. Boxes were also used for storing patches and small sweets or bonbons. Many of the boxes produced by the German factories were of simple rectangular or bombe form, but were invariably highly decorated, with finely painted panels of courtly ladies, hunting and shipping scenes or flowers. In England, simple shaped boxes were made, but usually in enamelled metal rather than porcelain.

Meissen thimble, c.1730

All these types of wares are extremely popular with collectors and indeed would have been collected from new for the fine quality and variety of decoration. They can also be easily displayed. Due to the popularity of collecting such wares they continued to be made in the 19th century, and many copies were made in 18th-century style, notably by Samson of Paris. Copies are generally not so finely painted, but as these wares are often unmarked and the undersides of pieces are usually decorated as well, they are often difficult to date and attribute.

Chelsea scent bottle, c.1751-4

Candlesticks and lighting

Ceramic candlesticks have been made since the beginning of the 18th century and fall into several distinct types:

• **Chambersticks:** These were carried to light a person's way to the bedroom, and because they were carried, these chambersticks usually have a distinctive loop handle, a wide tray and short nozzle. Many originally had a matching snuffer or extinguisher, of conical shape, which was kept on a cone-shaped fitting on the tray or handle when not in use.

Royal Worcester candle-snuffer, c.1910

• **Tapersticks:** Miniature candlesticks of 'traditional' shape. these were only 7.6–12.7cm (3–5in) high, with slender nozzles intended to hold a slender candle or taper to light a desk. Tapersticks are sometimes incorporated into inkstands.

• **Candlesticks:** Early shapes followed silver forms and they were invariably made in pairs or sets. A pair of candlesticks will always have considerably more value than a single one.

• **Dressing table candlesticks:** Dressing table sets were popular from the early 19th century to the 1920s and usually comprised a pair of candlesticks, perhaps 12.7–17.5cm (5–7in) high, several lidded pots, a stand for rings and a tray. Many such sets were produced by the Limoges and Staffordshire factories around 1900 and candlesticks from these sets are the most commonly seen ceramic candlesticks in antique shops and at fairs.

- **Candelabra:** Ornate candelabra with a central stem and four or more nozzles or lights were traditionally made in silver. German ceramic markers made elaborate versions in porcelain throughout the 19th century, the tall stems often modelled with figures and encrusted with flowers.
- **Candlesnuffers:** These were small hollow objects designed to be placed over a candle flame to extinguish it. Initially, the plain conical forms followed those of silver, but several factories in the 19th century, notably Royal Worcester, made novelty extinguishers of various shapes, often figural.

Meissen candlesticks, 19th century

It was not only candlesticks which were made of ceramic. Many oil lamps had decorative ceramic covers for the oil reservoirs. Ormolu ceiling candelabra often had ceramic sections and Wedgwood's jasperwares were often used for this purpose.

Garden, conservatory and exterior wares

In the 19th century, production methods allowed for the creation of larger and larger objects, and with the Victorian interest in the garden came a demand for large ceramic pieces for exterior and semi-exterior use. Garden seats in the shape of barrels were imported from China in the late 18th and early 19th centuries. They were copied by the Staffordshire potters in blue transfer-printed pearlware and later in majolica by Minton and his contemporaries. The Minton factory also used majolica as a medium for garden seats, large jardinieres, pedestals and even fountains.

Earthenware can suffer when used outside as water can enter the body through the glaze. A frost can then cause the water to freeze and expand, leading to flaking or lifting of the glaze and cracks.

Stoneware is a better medium for ware used outside; although less decorative, it is much less prone

Copeland majolica wall bracket, c.1875

to damage. Doulton made stoneware garden benches in the late 19th century, as well as large barrels and storage jars which could be kept safely outside or in damp cellars. Purely functional exterior items made in ceramic included telegraph pole insulators and water pipes.

Holdcroft majolica jardiniere, c.1875

Other functional wares

The range of objects made in pottery and porcelain is almost limitless and it is impossible to mention everything here. The following is a brief list and description of some other types of wares which are more frequently found.

Sanitary wares: The most commonly found are toilet sets, made for the bedroom and usually comprising jug, basin, chamber pot, water mug, soap box and cover, and toothbrush box and cover. Additional items may include a footbath, slop pail and sponge bowl and drainer. Before the advent of modern plumbing almost every home had at least one of these sets, and many survive today; chamber pots seem to survive in greater numbers than any other piece! Other sanitary wares were made and include the *bordalou* (female chamber pot), bed pans and toilet pans with elaborate blue printed decoration and sinks. Glazed earthenware or porcelain were ideal media for this type of ware as they could be easily cleaned.

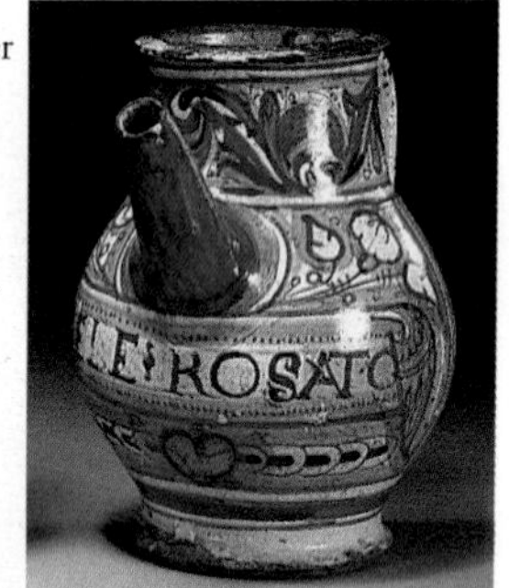

Italian maiolica wet drug jar, c.1500

Apothecary wares: Since the Middle Ages apothecaries had stored their medicines in pottery jars; to use maiolica or Delft was a natural progression. In Italy these jars are known as *albarelli.* The ones used for dry medicines are generally of simple waisted form with a grooved rim to allow a cloth cover to be fitted. Wet medicine jars tend to be footed, with a narrow neck and short spout for pouring. Such jars are usually inscribed with the name of the substance they were intended to hold and are often elaborately painted. Other apothecary wares include pill slabs, again usually found in Delft, as well as sets of jars made for chemists' shops. On a medical note, examples also exist of pottery and porcelain eye baths. These are extremely rare and avidly collected.

Other wares made from pottery or porcelain include such diverse items as: spittoons, tobacco jars, wig stands, water filters, carpet bowls and fireplace surrounds.

George Jomes toilet set, c.1870

Plaques and lithophanes

The subjects for plaques were often copies of old or contemporary masters, rarely originals, although extremely finely painted. This is more impressive when it is remembered that the colours used by the artist change in the firing. Portraits on porcelain were also popular, although often they were painted over a photographic image previously printed on to the porcelain as a guide.

Small plaques made of porcelain or jasperware, usually for mounting into furniture, were produced in the 18th century. Very small plaques and medallions were also made to be framed and hung, or mounted in jewellery. In the 19th century it became fashionable to have porcelain plaques resembling popular oil paintings. Early panels tended to be small as plain flat rectangles of porcelain were prone to warping in the kiln. As potters' techniques improved, larger panels were made, the most notable and finely painted coming from the factories of Berlin and Meissen in the second half of the 19th century.

German cup with lithophane base, 19th century

Earthenware plaques are more

unusual, but they do exist in pearlware, usually moulded in low relief and painted in Pratt colours with agricultural or figural subjects. Earthenware plaques were also sold undecorated, particularly in the late 19th century, to amateur painters. Collectors should be aware that these pieces, although bearing the factory mark of the maker, are not painted by a factory artist. Such amateur decorated wares, as they are known, are generally not collected and values for such pieces are usually low, no matter how decorative or well executed they may be.

Lithophanes are porcelain plaques thinly moulded with a design in intaglio. When held to a window or bulb, light transmitted through the areas of varying thickness brings out the detail of the subject. Lithophanes were first made at Meissen in the 1820s but were made by many different German factories throughout the 19th century. They were often mounted in stands before a window, but smaller panels could be set into the bases of cabinet cups. In the UK, the only major maker of lithophanes was the Belleek factory in Ireland. Lithophanes are rarely marked and are often difficult to date or attribute accurately.

Berlin plaque, 'Ruth', c.1870/80

Tiles

Tiles made of glazed earthenware originated from the Near East in pre-Christian times, where they were used as wall decorations.

In Europe, tiles first appear in the form of floor tiles in the medieval period and examples can be seen in many churches and cathedrals. Designs were either foliate or figural and either inlaid into the tile or painted in contrasting coloured slip on the surface. This tradition of tile-making gradually died out and it was not revived until the production of the first Delft wares, with tiles being used mainly for wall rather than floor decoration.

Despite an active English Delftware industry during the 18th century, thousands of Dutch Delft tiles were imported to England and many still survive. Purchase of a tile is the cheapest method of acquiring a piece of 18th-century English or Dutch Delft and examples of Dutch tiles can be found for few pounds. A few creamware tiles exist, and faience and lead-glazed tiles were used in Germany and other northern European countries on walls and on the exterior of stoves. Tile-making, however, reached its height in Victorian England.

Major English tile makers include: Minton, Copeland, Maw & Co., Craven Dunhill, Wedgwood, Pilkingtons, Poole and William de Morgan.

Tiles were used not only for interior decoration of walls and floors in public and private buildings, but were also used to make plant stands, flower boxes and fire surrounds. Tiled walls were as practical as they were easily cleaned, and the decoration was also permanently colourful. Decorative schemes include not only large expanses of geometric and foliate patterns and moulded textured tiles, but also large painted panels made up of numerous smaller tiles. Such panels are sometimes seen for sale, removed from their original setting. Many were made in sets which have now been split up.

Tiles form the subject matter of several specialist books, and the prospective collector should consult one of these to get some idea of the range of tiles made over the last three hundred years.

William de Morgan tiles, late 19th century

Figures

Actual figure models begin to appear made in Delftware, and later in salt-glazed stoneware, at first copying figures such as the small seated Buddhas imported from China.

No discussion of shapes would be complete without some mention of ceramic figure production. Images of people have been made in clay since the earliest times, often as symbols of fertility. In the medieval period in Europe there was relatively little figure modelling, with figure subjects only appearing in relief decoration on the surface of wares.

With the development of porcelain in Europe in the early 18th century, figure modelling began in earnest, and by the middle of the century figures were becoming the major production of many factories in England and on the Continent. Porcelain and fine earthenware with their thin glazes were far better suited to the fine detail needed in figure modelling than thickly tin-glazed earthenware. Indeed, even with a lead glaze, much detail is lost compared to the same model in biscuit state. This is partly why biscuit and parian were so popular for figure modelling.

- In England figures were used mainly for decoration around a room, standing on furniture pushed to the wall or on mantelpieces.
- Elsewhere in Europe figures were used as table decoration, and were modelled to be viewed 'in the round'.

- Subjects of figures were often taken from contemporary engravings and the way they were modelled derived partly from a tradition of stone sculpture and partly from a native tradition of wood carving.

Bow figures, c.1760-5

The following section briefly outlines the types of figures found in England and Germany:

ENGLISH POTTERY FIGURES

There are a limited number of surviving figures in white salt-glazed stoneware and Whieldon-type creamware, although they are rare and much sought after (and copied).

Subjects are usually courtly life, with models of ladies in voluminous dresses and figures of musicians. By the late 18th century, more and more figures, including copies of classical subjects, as well as rural and peasant figures, were being cheaply produced in creamware and pearlware. The pottery figure tradition in England has always tended to reflect contemporary life and in the 19th century, mass-produced figures were made as souvenirs of famous events. Up until about 1840 pottery figures tended to be modelled entirely in the round, either raised on a square classical-type base, or grassy mound with floral tree, known as a *bocage,* behind. During the 1840s, Staffordshire potters

Staffordshire pearlware Savoyard and bear group, c.1820

Staffordshire equestrian 'flatbacks', c.1860

moved away from this type of detail and began to model figures only partially in the round, so-called 'flatbacks'. Such figures were intended to stand on a mantelpiece against a chimney breast, so decoration and modelling of the back of the figure or group was not required.

This style of figure production continues today, with reproductions of late 19th-century figures continually appearing. They remain perennially popular and highly collectable, particularly those commemorating a specific event, since they would only have been made for a short period and for that reason are now quite rare.

ENGLISH PORCELAIN FIGURES

Porcelain figure production began in England in the 1750s, probably first at Chelsea and subsequently at Derby and Bow.

Other English factories produced some figures, but these three had the largest figural output. Subjects were copied from those used at Meissen and other German factories, as well as from imports from China. There was also interchange with the pottery figure makers.

English porcelain figures are usually of classical or allegorical subjects and were often made in sets with themes such as the four seasons, the elements, the five senses or the continents. Although early figures were free-standing, it became popular in the 1760s to add a floral *bocage* behind the figure for support and decoration, particularly at Chelsea and subsequently at Derby. Chelsea figures can be distinguished by the thick greenish glaze which has a tendency to pool, and by painted red or gold anchor marks. Derby figures were fired in the kiln on small balls of clay which when removed left

Derby figures, c.1765

small circular patches of unglazed body underneath the base, so-called 'patch marks'.

Figure production continued in the 19th century, although on a reduced scale, and subjects tended to become more contemporary. Parian became the preferred medium for larger figures. In this century, figure production has undergone a revival with factories such as Royal Doulton, Royal Worcester and Coalport producing large ranges of porcelain figures aimed at a collectors market.

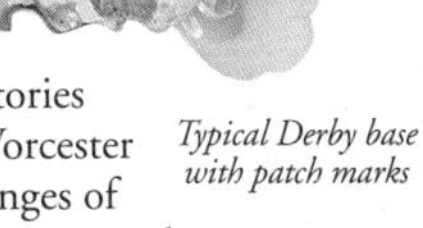

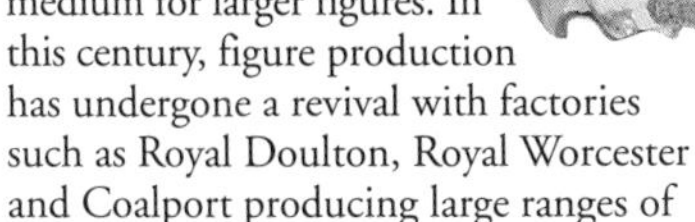

Typical Derby base with patch marks

GERMAN POTTERY AND PORCELAIN FIGURES

Although a limited number of pottery figures exist on the Continent. it is in porcelain that most figures were made, with Germany, and the Meissen factory in particular, leading the way.

The range of figures produced by the Meissen factory was vast. Beginning with small white porcelain models copied from imports from China, the factory soon became technically adept at making larger free-standing figures with the minimum of support. Figures were modelled in the round, and included sets of allegorical figures, complex groups and figures reflecting contemporary fashion and court life. Highly collectable figures include those of street vendors, the designs for the models taken from sets of 'Cries de Paris' engravings.

Meissen also produced a much imitated set of anthropomorphical figures of monkey bandsmen, each playing a different musical instrument, a full set including female singers and a conductor. Such figures are still produced by Meissen today.

Eighteenth-century Meissen figures can be distinguished by their flat unglazed bases and small blue crossed swords mark at the back of the figure near the base. Such figures were much copied by other 18th-century factories and 19th-century fakers such as Samson in Paris.

Meissen 'monkey bandsmen', 19th century

In the 19th century the Meissen factory produced extremely well-modelled figures and groups, some of enormous size and complexity. These later figures are glazed underneath, the crossed swords mark is usually accompanied by incised and impressed numerals. Meissen continues to make figures today, including contemporary designs as well as copies of 18th- and 19th-century models.

Elsewhere in Germany and the rest of Continental Europe during the late 19th century, figures were made by many factories. Often these figures were of relatively poor quality and were made in large numbers. In Dresden prior to World War II, figures of dancers in lace costume were popular, as well as cheaply produced and crudely modelled coloured bisque porcelain figures of children, often in saccharine sweet pale yellow and blue colouring. Most of these later figures are of relatively low value as they were produced (and survived) in large numbers.

Meissen 19th-century figure groups

INFLUENCES 

Introduction

From the previous sections it will be clear that the design of European ceramics did not simply evolve from a native tradition, but was heavily influenced by the ceramics of other, more distant countries. The following pages will look at the influence of China, Japan and the Islamic countries in this respect.

Influence on design was not just restricted to examples of work in the same media. Potters did not work in isolation for an exclusive market, and often they were in competition, particularly with silver and metal smiths. Pewter and, latterly, silver, were the favoured materials of food- and drink-related wares, particularly with the more wealthy. The products of the new porcelain manufacturers in the 18th century were in direct competition with those of the silversmiths, and ceramic manufacturers frequently attempted to emulate complex silver shapes.

The last pages of this section look at sources of decoration, other than Oriental and Eastern. Potters needed their decoration to appear sophisticated and interesting to appeal to their wealthy buyers, and they frequently turned to printmakers for inspiration. Prints could be cheaply purchased and reproduced and the ceramic painters had only to copy the design on to the ware, rather than think about composition and perspective. Prints were also used as sources for the complex engraved blue and white transfer printed wares of the early 19th century.

Exchanges of ideas between ceramic manufacturers and designers accustomed to working in other areas often achieve good quality results. Just two more recent examples of the cross-over of designers to ceramics from a different media or discipline can be seen in the work of Dr Christopher Dresser who worked for Minton and Linthorpe in the 1870s–80s, and Keith Murray who designing for Wedgwood in the 1930s–40s.

- **Christopher Dresser:** A botanist who had a strong interest in Japanese design and he combined the two to produce stunning formalized patterns for Minton, and extremely unusual organic shapes with monochrome glazes for Linthorpe. Interestingly, he also designed wallpaper, fabric, furniture, glass and silver.
- **Keith Murray:** Trained as an architect in the 1920s and designed a series of simple and elegant vases and bowls in solid matt colours for Wedgwood. He also worked in glass, designing shapes and engraved surface decoration.

Minton spill vase, design by Dresser, c.1880

China

The influence of China in Europe was strong in several ways, not least by inspiring the development of porcelain. Influence on shape and decoration of wares was equally important. Decoration directly inspired by Chinese colour palettes and subjects included: *famille rose,* a palette of coloured enamels including rose pink, and *famille vert,* a similar palette, lacking pink, but included a brilliant green enamel.

Floral patterns in these colour schemes made use of Oriental plants such as peony, prunus (plum blossom), pine and bamboo. These same subjects, along with figural ones, were also painted on to underglaze-blue and white wares. Shapes are less easy to place, but plain cylinders and balusters derive from Chinese originals. Most factories' figure ranges also included Oriental

English teapot with Chinese-style decoration, c.1770

figures. Other wares besides porcelain which were copied included red stoneware (Yixing ware) and relief moulded white wares from Fujian Province.

> In the early part of this century cheaply made imports from China and Japan became popular with the working and middle classes and Staffordshire potters, in particular, responded by mass producing wares in similar style, often rather poorly made.

Initially these wares were copied by European potters as best they could, and the decoration was sometimes rather oddly interpreted. In the 1730s–40s, factories such as Meissen began to make direct copies of, and replacements for, Chinese originals.

In the 19th century imports from China began to decline and native European wares became more popular. The Chinese influence continued, with many Oriental floral patterns, particularly on ironstone dinner services, and with Oriental-style blue and white printed patterns such as the willow pattern. These types of Chinese-inspired patterns are known as **chinoiserie.**

Chinese exportware, c.1800

Japan

Imports from Japan appeared in Europe in the early to mid-17th century when Chinese imports stopped due to internal political problems. Japanese wares also became popular again when Japan was opened to the west in the 1860s. In the early period the main influence from Japan was, as with China, the decorative schemes and colour palettes used on the wares.

Kakiemon was a palette of predominantly blue, green and orange colours, used sparingly for simple patterns which European potters could easily copy. *Imari,* named after the port from which the wares were imported, is a palette of

Japanese Imari, Meiji period (1868–1912)

underglaze-blue, orange-iron red and gold. Patterns tend to be all over and highly stylized. Plants are sometimes recognizable, but formal patterned borders predominate. These patterns are often referred to in Europe as 'Japan' patterns.

The Japanese influence reappeared strongly in the 19th century with the so-called Aesthetic Movement. The Japanese combination of formal pattern with realistic representation of nature was extremely influential. Also popular were the gilding and bronzing of ceramics in imitation of Japanese metalwork. Even carved ivory was simulated in porcelain. Examples of this late influence can be seen in the productions of the Royal Worcester factory during this period.

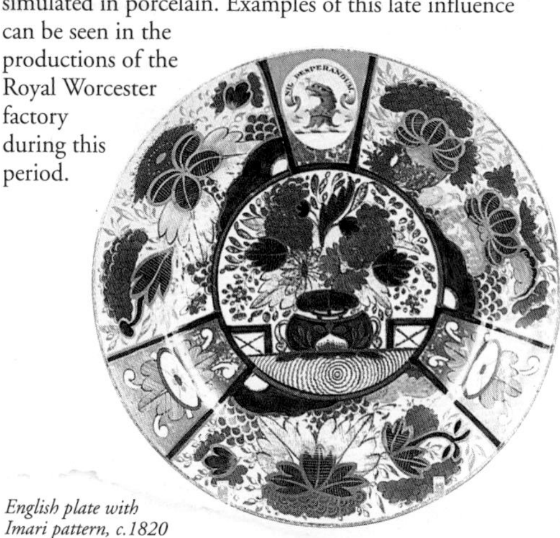

English plate with Imari pattern, c.1820

Islam

During the 14th and 15th centuries the influence of the Islamic world was strong in Italy and Spain, but elsewhere in Europe, China and Japan were always more important as a design influence. In the 19th century, the interest in Islamic designs increased, partly due to the many large international exhibitions where the designs of the Islamic countries would be displayed, and partly due to the increased number of people travelling to these countries.

Many factories produced close replicas of Islamic designs which are much sought after by collectors of Islamic-style wares today. The Cantagalli factory in Italy was one such, producing chargers, mugs and vases. European factories also made Islamic style wares for sale in those countries, and prominent Islamic figures commissioned European factories to create services with Islamic inscriptions and crests.

Shapes of Islamic wares were also influential, including slender-necked bottle vases. The patterns of much-pierced or reticulated decoration derived from Islamic prototypes. In the late 19th century the influences of Islam and Japan were often combined to produce many exotically coloured and shaped wares.

William De Morgan 'Persian' bowl, c.1890

Metalwork

When the first porcelain factories started in the early to mid-18th century they tended to look to metalwork as their inspiration for shapes, and in some cases employed former silversmiths in their factories. An example of this was at Chelsea in England where Nicholas Sprimont, a silversmith from Liège, worked first as a factory manager from 1749, and after 1758 as proprietor. Silverware supplied not only basic shapes of ware but also elements of decoration. Scroll moulding,

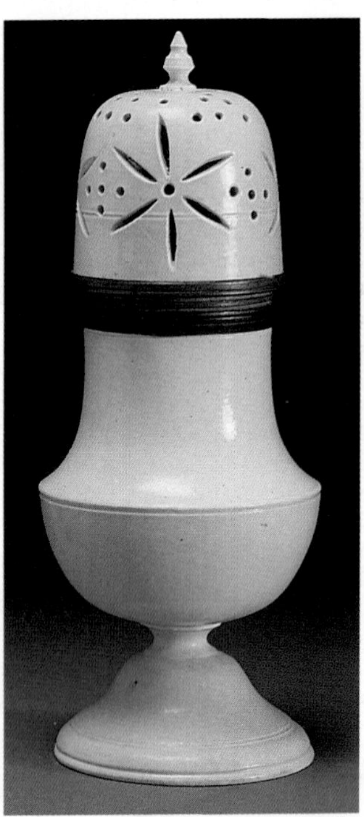

Salt-glaze stoneware, c.1750/60

gadrooning and reeded borders are all derived from metalwork.

Initially shapes were direct copies but it soon became clear that the production of certain shapes was not suited to such a different media. Tea canisters, for example, were initially rectangular, built from four slabs of clay. Such upright flat areas of clay had a tendency to warp and it was realized that tea canisters were more practically made in an ovoid shape.

Later in the 19th century, potters moved further away from metalwork prototypes and began to experiment with other forms. The inspiration from metalwork remained and continued into this century. Clarice Cliff, the most collected of British Art Deco designers, used the silver designs of Jean Tetard as the basis for her angular 'Stamford' and circular 'Bonjour' shaped teapots.

Silver sugar sifter, 1750

Prints and paintings

Although Chinese and Japanese ceramics were a major source of inspiration for European potters, an equally valuable source was contemporary engraving. Mass-produced engraved prints of Old Masters and contemporary painters were widely and cheaply available. Printed wares often followed these sources, and on painted wares they were adapted and interpreted to fit the shape of the object and skill of the artist.

Series of prints of distant lands were used by the makers of blue and white transfer printed wares in the early 19th century, as were sets of engravings of British country houses. Books of botanical studies with printed or painted illustrations were also popular at this period, and influenced potters to produce finely painted botanical subjects on pottery and porcelain. It can be eminently satisfying to track down or stumble across the printed or painted source of a ceramic design and, although many have been traced, much work still remains to be done.

Staffordshire meat dish transfer-printed after an engraving, c.1830

HISTORICAL SURVEY

Introduction

The first three chapters look at ceramics generally, classified according to body, decoration and function, while the fourth has examined some of the influences on the development of European ceramics. The following pages highlight some of the major European factories and designers in more detail. This section is by no means comprehensive, and there will be many factories not included. Those which have been included are arguably the most important and have had the most influence over the production of others.

As well as factories this chapter includes sections on particular periods or movements, such as the Empire style in France where, although the individual factories are less important, the combined output is significant. The factories appear in alphabetical order within each section. Again, it must be stressed that although these are key factories, the list is by no means comprehensive. The marks of these and many other important factories are listed in the compendium. These marks will help with identification of wares, and the bibliography should be used to find out more about makers not discussed here. Also listed are some of the commonly found marks of makers with large, but perhaps less influential productions. Not all of these are discussed in detail; however, some were large-scale producers and are often collectable today.

Each factory is discussed giving dates and major landmarks of production. For the sake of convenience the section is divided into three, with a brief discussion of style and areas not necessarily covered by specific makers, followed by Continental, and then English makers and movements, arranged in alphabetical order.

European Vienna-style vases, c.1900

European pottery before 1800

Most of the earthenwares produced in Europe prior to 1800 fall into areas already discussed in the chapters on type and body. Wares tended to be made in localized centres, and ceramic factories, in the modern sense, did not exist until the 18th century, and then in Europe particularly, only for the production of the new material porcelain. The following pages briefly summarize the pottery produced in Europe before 1800.

English Delftware plate, c.1740

England

In England the medieval tradition of simple lead-glazed wares gave way first to the more decorative slipwares, and then to Delftware. Medieval production tended to be localized, with small groups of individual potters working in the region of a good clay deposit. The production of slipware was similarly concentrated, and particularly strong in Staffordshire and the West Country. Delftware makers tended to be located in major cities or ports, notably London, Liverpool and Bristol.

Germany

The earliest earthenwares in Germany were also lead-glazed. Unlike in England, this tradition gave way to the production of stonewares with salt glazes towards the end of the 14th century.

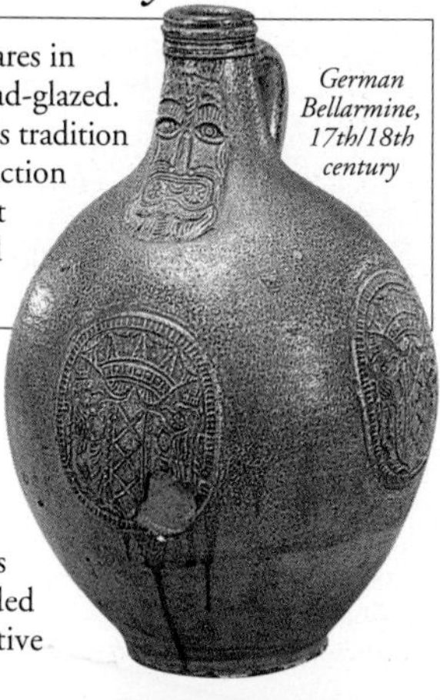

German Bellarmine, 17th/18th century

Major centres of production were Siegburg, Frenchen, Raeren and Cologne, and each, although producing similar wares with incised and moulded decoration, had distinctive styles. Characteristic of Cologne is the *bartmanskrug*, a jug which has a moulded or incised face beneath the spout. Traditionally, this face is supposed to be that of Cardinal Bellarmino, a Catholic opposed to the reformed church of the Protestant countries, and such jugs have become known by the name Bellarmine, although the tradition of such decoration is known much earlier. Bellarmine jugs were also made in England in the late 17th century as the stoneware tradition began. Examples, although similar to German ones, are much rarer.

The stoneware tradition in Germany continues to the present day, but parallel to it in the late 17th and 18th centuries was the production of tin-glazed earthenware or faience. Wares were similar to those made in England and Holland at the same period, with blue and white decoration predominant.

Italy

The very earliest Italian earthenwares grew out of the products of antiquity; they were initially lead-glazed and similar to many northern European objects.

By the 14th century, two distinct types were emerging: slipwares, usually with incised decoration, and tin-glazed earthenwares, or maiolica. Maiolica was produced in several regions of Italy, with each area having a distinctive style, usually in the subject matter of the decoration or the colour palette.

On many earlier wares decoration was often simple

painted stylized foliage or primitive figures and animals. More complex subjects soon appeared, including portraits, usually in profile, armorials, and, in the early 16th century, *istoriato* subjects. *Istoriato* wares were painted entirely with storytelling scenes, usually biblical or mythological and frequented by numerous figures against a landscape or architectural background. Such wares, particularly dishes which display the subject matter to the best advantage, are now extremely collectable and sell for thousands of pounds.

The maiolica tradition continued into the 19th century and exists today, with many copies of early wares being made, an important point to remember when trying to identify and date a piece.

Urbino maiolica, dated 1542

France

The earliest pottery wares produced in France were simple vessels of lead-glazed earthenware. Indeed these types of wares continue to be produced today.

There were two specific types of pottery produced in France worthy of further discussion: the lead-glazed wares of Bernard Palissy; and the tradition of faience or tin-glazed earthenware which continues today.

Palissy was working in the mid-16th century and to him is attributed (perhaps erroneously), a group of colourful lead-glazed earthenwares moulded with naturalistic subjects such as shells, plants, fish and lizards. Such wares are rare and much copied, particularly by Portuguese potters in the 19th century.

French faience or tin-glazed earthenware developed in the late 16th century from early Italian maiolica-style wares. Various regions and towns in France developed similar wares with a very white tin-glaze, but each decorated these wares in a style peculiar to their particular region. Main centres included Strasbourg, Rouen, Quimper and Moustiers. Sometimes difficult to date accurately, these wares were decorated in a similar way through out the 18th century and into the 19th century; similar wares are still produced at Quimper today.

Palissy-type dish, early 17th century

Porcelain before 1800

> It must be remembered that the early factories were experimenting and that successful results were sometimes a long time coming. It helped to have a royal patron and plenty of financial backing, but even the most successful factories went through lean periods, and this has sometimes been reflected in the quality of work produced.

How porcelain was developed in Europe, and what influenced the shapes and decoration of the early wares has already been discussed. The following pages look at key factories which appeared during this period, including more experimental factories which survived

Vauxhall porcelain bottles, c.1755–60

only a few years, and those which thrived and are still on-going, both in England and the rest of Europe.

Most key factories are detailed, but it is virtually impossible to mention them all. Some were very short-lived, and little is known except for the attributed surviving wares, usually unmarked during this early period. It should be possible to see examples of the work of most of the factories mentioned in museums, or to handle pieces for sale at antiques fairs and auctions.

Meissen 'Swan service' plate, 18th century, with swan detail in centre

The 19th century

The variety of wares produced during the 19th century was almost endless and this period produced not only innovation but also reproductions, as many makers looked to the 18th century and earlier for inspiration.

The 19th century was the age of industrialization and inevitably, the working methods of the ceramic industry altered during this period. Some factories which had been important in the 18th century disappeared, or were taken over, while others went from strength to strength. Towards the end of the century, industrialization began to have more of an effect on the works produced and many new factories sprang up in Staffordshire and on the Continent, producing lower-quality mass-produced wares for the rapidly increasing population.

High-quality hand-painted wares were produced in the early 19th century in England by the Worcester factories, at Derby and at Coalport, for instance. These Regency period wares were matched on the Continent by the French and Bohemian makers of Neo-classical and Empire period porcelains. The copious use of high quality gilding was a notable feature of all quality wares of the period.

The late 19th century saw the appearance of more 'art' potteries, working outside the now traditional factory environment and following the principles of simple form and function laid down by William Morris and his contemporaries. The products of these makers were popular, and during this period many of the larger factories began to produce Arts and Crafts 'art' ranges. These ceramic productions formed part of a larger Arts and Crafts movement parallel to and, in some cases, part of what is now termed Art Nouveau.

The effect of Japan and the Orient on design in the 1870s–80s has already been mentioned, and many 19th-century makers produced so-called Aesthetic Movement wares.

Staffordshire Aesthetic Movement majolica jug, c.1870/80

Art Nouveau

The makers of ceramics at this period were many and not all work was modern and Art Nouveau in style. Some continued to use rather traditional floral designs and even looked back to rococo and Neo-classical designs for inspiration, ignoring the general Art Nouveau principle of adherence to nature and the rejection of antiquity.

The term Art Nouveau was first used in the 1880s to describe the modern works in all media being produced at that period. Latterly, it has been used rather indiscriminately as a blanket name to describe a period of several rather different styles of design prevalent on the Continent and in England from the late 1880s to the beginning of the so-called Art Deco period in the 1920s.

These include the sinuous and stylized plant-like designs epitomized by Hector Guimard in his designs for the entrances to the Paris Metro; the geometric designs of the Secessionist Movement in Austria in the late 1800s; International Modernism; and the sometimes rather austere designs of Charles Rennie Mackintosh and the Glasgow School.

Mintons Secessionist ware, c.1905

The latter was a development of the British Arts and Crafts movement. The ceramics of this period often show the influence of one or more of these movements in their design, in the design of shape as well as surface decoration.

Royal Dux sweetmeat figure, c.1910

Art Deco

The term Art Deco is now accepted as a descriptive name of the modern designs produced in the mid-1920s and into the 1930s. The designs popularly associated with Art Deco are the simple lines and curves of the Odeon cinemas and the bright colours used by the ceramic designer Clarice Cliff. What is now termed Art Deco partly developed as a reaction to the over-stylized forms of Art Nouveau, and Art Deco designs overall tend to be simpler and brighter, although in the 1930s muted shades of green and beige became more popular.

Both Art Nouveau and Art Deco are periods of design which have been written about extensively and there is not enough space here to go into more detail, other than to list in the following sections some of the more commonly found factories and designers, and their wares.

There is often confusion between what constitutes Art Nouveau or Art Deco design; the following points are intended as a simple guide.

Clarice Cliff 'Tennis' pattern teapot, c.1931

Clarice Cliff 'Farmhouse' pattern jug, c.1931/2

Art Nouveau or Art Deco?

The points below do not apply just to ceramics, but can also be looked for in other media. Ability to recognize what is Art Nouveau or Art Deco can help with dating and attribution of an object.

- Art Nouveau designs are often plant-based and make use of flowing curves and sinuous whiplash motifs.
- Art Deco designs tend to be more angular, using simple combinations of geometric shapes, triangles, rectangles and semi-circles.
- Art Nouveau colours are often soft and natural – green, violet, pink and peach are popular.
- Art Deco colours are generally bold – orange, bright blue, purple and yellow. Striking combinations of light and dark colours were also popular, as were more muted shades of green and beige in the 1930s.
- Popular Art Nouveau motifs include stylized flowerheads and seed pods, female figures with flowing drapery and long hair, tall stemmed plants,

Clarice Cliff 'Melon' Art Deco plate, c.1930/1

waterlilies and poppies. Secessionist and Modernist wares make use of similar subjects treated in a simple, generally more angular and highly stylized manner.

- Popular Art Deco motifs include the sunburst or rising sun, rounded simple flowerheads or arrangements of flowers, triangular motifs and stylized animals, including the ubiquitous leaping deer.

Staffordshire Art Nouveau-style jug, c.1910

The war years

Even after World War II came to an end in 1945 it was some time before decorative production began again, and new designs did not really start to appear until the 1950s. Hence wares of the 1940s are not discussed; in many ways, quite literally, they do not exist.

The terms Art Deco and Art Nouveau are familiar to most people and both periods produced work which is highly collectable. Another period which is gaining in popularity is the 1950s, but before discussing this decade some mention must be made of the war years.

The Art Deco era effectively came to an end in 1939 with the outbreak of World War II. Shortly afterwards, in England at least, decorative ceramic production all but ceased. Wares for the home market in England had to be white, plain, simple and cost effective. A limited amount of decorative ware was made, but only for export, and the designs tended to be those of the 1930s. A whole section of the workforce went off to fight and designers' talents were employed elsewhere.

The outbreak of war and the cessation of decorative production also meant that some items of the late 1930s are quite rare. While some designs and shapes reappeared after the war, others did not and so were only in production for a short time. An example of this is a set of nursery ware figures of rabbits (Bunnykins) produced by Royal Doulton in 1939. These five figures were not made after the war and the limited number of sets sold in 1939 have become highly collectable, although they were relatively inexpensive figures, originally intended for mass production.

Royal Doulton 'Farmer Bunnykin', c.1939

The 1950s and after

Ceramics from the 1950s, 1960s and 1970s are only just beginning to be collected and so far few reference books exist.

After World War II it was several years before ceramic manufacturers began to produce new designs. In Britain, the 1951 Festival of Britain inspired designers to create innovative work, as did the yearly British Industry Fairs. Some factories employed designers from other fields to produce modern ceramic designs. Midwinter was a particularly successful example of this, employing amongst others Hugh Casson and Jessie Tait.

Susie Cooper continued to produce her own wares, with bone china

Ridgway 'Homemaker', • 1950s

gradually taking over from earthenware. After her takeover by Wedgwood in the 1960s she produced a striking range of simple designs known as 'Contrast'. Another easily recognized and collectable pattern from this period is Ridgway's 'Homemaker', a black printed design of 1950s-style domestic objects including a kidney-shaped coffee table, a television and items of cutlery. This was retailed through Woolworths.

Look out for good strong designs (printed or painted) and particular shapes and patterns which can be immediately associated with those periods. These should become the collectable antiques of the future.

Susie Cooper bone china, from the 'Contrast' range, 1960s

Studio pottery and porcelain

The work of the studio potters is essentially a development of the work of the art potters of the 19th century. Potters such as the Martin Brothers and William Howson Taylor were experimenting with glaze effects and looking to the Orient for influence, but their productions were still on a relatively large scale. It was with the arrival of Bernard Leach to Britain from Japan in 1920 that the studio pottery movement began.

CHARACTERISTICS OF STUDIO POTTERY

- Hand-built or hand-thrown wares.
- Decoration achieved often by glaze alone.

Bernard Leach and studio pottery wares, 20th century

- Strong, simple architectural or organic shapes.
- Pre-1950s, mostly stoneware or earthenware; 1950s onwards experiments with porcelain.
- Strong Oriental influence, particularly Bernard Leach and his followers.
- Marks are usually stamped or impressed (seal marks), or painted initials.

The most important and collected studio potters were and are working in Britain. Only in Japan were there works produced of comparable quality. Detailed below are some of the more influential studio potters:

BERNARD LEACH (1887–1979), SHOJI HAMADA (1894–1978) AND ST IVES

Bernard Leach and Shoji Hamada worked together in Japan in the 1910s and founded a pottery at St Ives in 1920. They produced stoneware and slipware influenced by native British pottery and Japanese tradition. Importantly, they looked at their pots as a whole, not just in terms of surface decoration, and the materials and glazes were of prime importance. The St Ives pottery attracted and influenced a number of other potters including Leach's son, David and wife, Janet. Leach continued to work and teach mostly in Britain, while Hamada was based in Japan and toured the USA, but sold many pots through St Ives. Leach's early work is mostly stoneware and earthenware, and later porcelain. St Ives produced a range of domestic wares designed by Leach and some pieces can be purchased relatively inexpensively.

MICHAEL CARDEW (1901–83)

A student of Bernard Leach, Michael Cardew worked predominantly in slipware at Wenford Bridge, Winchcombe and Abuja in Nigeria. He is known for earthenware and stonewares.

LUCIE RIE (1902–95) AND HANS COPER (1920–81)

Both Rie and Coper were influential post-war studio potters. Lucie Rie worked in Vienna prior to World War II making simple earthenware pots with 'volcanic' glazes. Her post-war work became more refined and sculptural, unlike Leach's rather rustic approach. She worked with Hans Coper from 1946 and they tended to work mostly in fine stoneware and porcelain with complex high temperature glazes. Joint Coper-Rie works were produced in the 1950s bearing both their marks. Coper was an influential teacher in the 1960s of many contemporary studio potters.

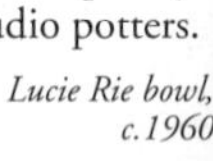

Lucie Rie bowl, c.1960

ELIZABETH FRITSCHE (1940–)

An influential studio potter during the 1970s–80s, Fritsche works in coloured clays and slips. She is noted for decorative rather than functional works, with shapes often flattened and barely three-dimensional, geometric patterns.

Elizabeth Fritsche vase, c.1975

Continental factories, designers and movements

BERLIN

Royal porcelain factory 1763 to the present day. It produced fine quality tablewares and figures up to the end of the 18th century and large decorative vases made in the Empire style in the early-19th century. Figure and service production also continued. This factory was known for fine quality painted plaques and lithophanes.

BOHEMIA

The area now known as the Czech Republic has a strong tradition of porcelain production. In the 19th century various makers produced boldly painted wares with a very white glassy porcelain body, sometimes confused with Paris porcelains.

CHANTILLY

This porcelain factory was founded by Louis-Henri de Bourbon, Prince de Condé, in 1725. The main factory continued until the end of the century. It was known for early, unusual tin-glazed porcelain superseded by soft paste

Chantilly 'kakiemon' pattern, c.1730

porcelain *c.*1750. Its most characteristic decoration is in *kakiemon* palette with direct copies of Japanese patterns produced. It is also noted for limited figure production.

COPENHAGEN

Royal Porcelain factory 1775 to the present day. Bing & Grondahl 1850s to the present day. Both factories were known for figure modelling in biscuit in the 19th century, and later for glazed porcelain figures with distinctive grey-blue-green colouring. Royal Cophenhagen still produces copies of its famous *Flora Danica* service, originally made for the Russian Empress Catherine II.

Royal Copenhagen 'Flora Danica', 20th century

DRESDEN

This German city has numerous porcelain factories and decorating studios. It is noted for late 19th-century floral wares produced by several factories in similar style. 'Dresden porcelain' was the old fashioned way of describing Meissen, but is now used to describe wares in Meissen-style but not from the factory.

Dresden bottle vase, c.1880

FRANKENTHAL

Founded in 1755 by Paul-Antoine Hannong and closed in 1799, this factory produced hard paste porcelain. It is best known for fine quality figure production.

FURSTENBURG

Founded in 1747 by Duke Carl I of Brunswick, this factory flourished from 1770 to the early 19th century, and continues today. It is known for figures modelled by Simon Feilner, and has a large output of tablewares with distinctive moulded borders.

GARDNER

Francis Gardner worked in Moscow from 1766 onwards. He is best known for figures, mostly of Russian peasant-type, but also some fine quality services.

JACOB PETIT

From 1790 to the late 19th century, this factory produced typical Paris porcelains. Noted for white, glassy hard paste body. Flourished around 1840, producing figural scent bottles, clock cases and related highly decorative wares.

LIMOGES

Numerous porcelain factories and decorating studios were centred around this French town. Wares most commonly seen include dessert services and dressing table sets, mostly made around 1890–1910.

LUDWIGSBURG

Founded in 1758 by decree of Duke Carl Eugen von Württemberg; closed 1824. Noted for greyish coloured hard paste body. Early figures were produced in rococo style, developing into a classical style. It also produced some tablewares and ornamental forms.

Ludwigsburg figure group, c.1770/80

MEISSEN

Factory founded in the early 1700s by Augustus the Strong of Saxony. Johann Friedrich Bottger produced the first true porcelain around 1710. Meissen is the single most important German factory in terms of ceramic history and it would be impossible to do justice to its vast output within this book. Meissen is influential in both figure and tableware manufacture. The factory continues today.

Meissen coffee pot, c.1725

NYMPHENBURG

Founded *c.*1753 and continues today, it produces fine white porcelain. Noted for figure productions, exact replicas of which are still produced by the factory today; 19th-century copies also exist. Franz Anton Bustelli was the chief figure modeller 1754–63. Also produced tablewares.

PARIS

Numerous porcelain manufacturers and, more importantly, decorating studios were based here, particularly in the 19th century. Some of the finest quality Neo-classical and Empire porcelains can be attributed to the numerous Paris decorators.

ROYAL DUX

Bohemian factory noted for its distinctive figure production *c.*1900. Modelled either naturalistically or in Art Nouveau style, its wares are coloured in shades of green, pink and cream with gilt detail.

SAMSON

Edme Samson founded his works in Paris *c.*1845 and continued until about 1900. He made copies and imitations of porcelain and tin-glazed ware. Numerous fake marks as well as distinctive Samson marks exist. Porcelain tends to be hard and glassy, and figures lack exact detail of the originals.

SÈVRES AND VINCENNES

National porcelain manufacturer of France, established *c.*1738 at Vincennes, and from 1756 at Sèvres. Noted for table wares with distinctive blue, turquoise and pink grounds. Numerous services made under royal patronage. Sèvres is a difficult factory to study as its wares have been extensively copied. In the late 18th and early 19th centuries, many factory-produced wares were sold in the white (not decorated), and were subsequently decorated, adding to the confusion. The factory continues today.

SITZENDORF

Founded in 1850, the factory here continues today. Its most recognized productions are copies of Meissen produced in the second half of the 19th century, ranging

Sèvres ice pail, c.1760, with later decoration

from single figures to large candelabra. Many pieces have flower-encrusted decoration.

VIENNA

Du Paquier was experimenting with porcelain in 1718, and in 1744 it was taken over by the Austrian state; closed 1864. It was known for finely painted early 18th-century tablewares, but later 18th-century wares were less inventive. During the late 18th and early 19th centuries, it produced finely painted and gilt tablewares which have been extensively copied.

Vienna cabaret service, c.1800

British and Irish factories, designers and styles

BELLEEK

Founded 1863 and continues today; its notable wares include fine egg-shell porcelain teawares, often modelled in the form of shells, lithophanes, baskets and parian figures.

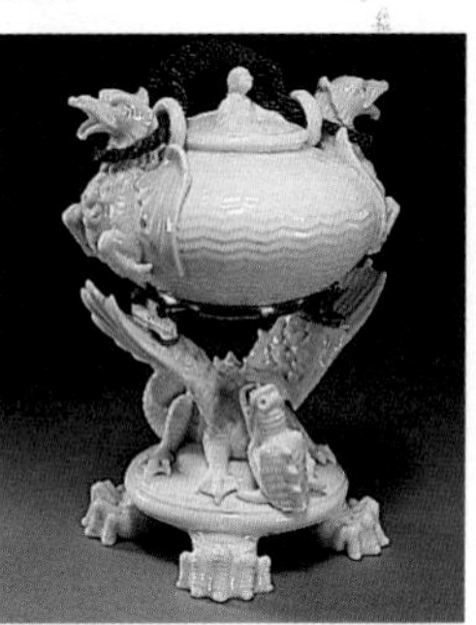
Belleek tea kettle and stand, c.1870

BOW

One of the earliest English porcelain factories *c.*1747–76, Bow made wares in Chinese style. Noted also for figure production.

CAUGHLEY

Shropshire factory founded by Thomas Turner, and existed from *c.*1775–99. Made wares in the style of the Worcester factory. Its decoration was predominantly underglaze-blue, printed and painted; also known as 'salopian' ware. Produced service and tablewares almost exclusively.

CHELSEA

In operation from 1745–69, it was run by silversmith Nicholas Sprimont. The factory made mostly polychrome-decorated decorative ware, including large vases and many different figures. 'Toys' were also made. The factory was eventually sold and in 1770 was taken over by William Duesbury of the Derby factory. So-called Chelsea-Derby wares were made between 1770–84.

CLARICE CLIFF

Designer working for Wilkinsons Ltd from the early 1920s. In 1928 she was given the task of decorating a group of old-fashioned blanks which had been acquired when Wilkinsons took over the nearby Newport pottery. She painted these wares in bright colours and geometric patterns, a range which was known as 'Bizarre'. She became the chief designer, producing a further range known as 'Fantasque'. By the late 1930s she virtually stopped designing, but all of the factories' wares continued to bear her name into the late 1950s.

Clarice Cliff 'Applique' ware vase, c.1930

COALPORT AND COALBROOKDALE

Established in 1795 and continuing to the present day. The earliest Coalport manufacturer was called John Rose and his opposition was a partnership called Anstice, Horton & Rose. This was dissolved in 1814 and John

Rose took over the running of both factories. The factory has always produced high quality wares, but is best known for its flower-encrusted ware of the period 1820–40, which is sometimes described as Coalbrookdale porcelain. In 1926 the factory moved from Shropshire to Staffordshire.

SUSIE COOPER

Designer working for A. E. Gray & Co. until 1928 when she set up her own factory. This factory continued despite setbacks until the 1960s when she was taken over by the Wedgwood group. She continued to produce designs until the 1980s. She died in 1995. Her motto was 'elegance and utility' and she combined traditionalism with Art Deco to create functional, well-designed tablewares. Her vases and non-tablewares are relatively unusual.

DAVENPORT

Operating from 1793 to 1887, this pottery factory was initially run by John Davenport at Longport in Staffordshire. It also produced porcelains. Notable wares

Susie Cooper 'Dresden' spray tea wares, 1930s

are fine pearlwares with printed or painted decoration; porcelain ornamental and dessert wares are also of high quality. Unusually for a factory of this period, ware is invariably marked.

DERBY

Operating from 1750 to the present day, the factory has been though numerous partnerships and working periods. It eventually became Royal Crown Derby in the 1890s. Early work included figure and tablewares, as well as ornamental vases, and the factory continued to produced an extremely wide range of ware in the 19th century. Pieces from the period 1890–1930 are of particularly fine quality and tend to be widely collected. Best known for their hand-painted *Imari* pattern wares still produced today.

Royal Crown Derby vases, late 19th century and early 20th century

DOULTON

John Doulton and John Watts began a stoneware business in Lambeth in 1815. This gradually developed, mainly due to the input of Henry Doulton, and the business also had a factory at Burslem in Staffordshire from 1882. From 1956 onwards all ware has been made at Burslem.

Royal Doulton series ware jug, 1920s

Known for stonewares designed by Hannah Barlow and George Tinworth, and a range of art wares developed by Charles Noke from the late 19th century onwards. Its mass-produced series ware from the early 20th century is widely collected today, as are the numerous figures and character jugs, which are still produced. Now also a notable tableware factory.

MARTIN BROTHERS

Working in Fulham from 1873 to 1914, four brothers – Robert, Edwin, Walter and Charles – made art pottery in stoneware. They were known for their models of grotesque birds and animals, and also for decorative ware with incised decoration.

MASON'S

Initially a porcelain factory run by Miles Mason from 1796–97. In 1813, Charles James Mason registered a patent for Ironstone China and this ware dominated production. The name Masons survives today but the factory has been taken over numerous times. It is known for the durable ironstone wares, both table and ornamental, usually with Oriental-style patterns.

Martin Brothers bird jar, c.1890

MINTON

Founded by Thomas Minton in 1793 and still operating today. The period 1850–1900 was dominated by Herbert Minton and the wares from this period are probably the best known. Produced majolica and porcelain wares, all highly decorated. After 1873 the factory became known as Mintons.

Minton plate, c.1870

MOORCROFT

William Moorcroft was a designer who worked for James Macintyre and Co. from the late 19th century until 1913 when he established his own pottery which continues today. All wares have distinctive tube-lined decoration. Early wares were retailed through Liberty & Co. Modern wares as well as pre-war wares are extremely collectable.

WILLIAM DE MORGAN

Designer and decorator working mainly on blanks in the period 1872– 1907, producing lustre wares and Persian-style wares,

Vase designed by Moorcroft for Macintyre, c.1900

with very complex patterns showing strong Italian renaissance influence. Wares are extremely collectable. Also produced tiles.

PILKINGTONS

Pilkingtons Royal Lancastrian 1893–1938, was best known for high-quality lustre-decorated wares, but also produced tiles and monochrome glazed wares.

Pilkingtons Royal Lancastrian vase, c.1910

POOLE

Dorset pottery originally known as Carter, Stabler and Adams after the main partners, it produced wares from the 1920s to the present day. Best known are its later wares painted with stylized flowers in purple, pink, yellow and green on a cream ground. Early wares as well as the brightly coloured 'Aegean' range from the 1970s are avidly collected.

Poole vase, 1930s

ROCKINGHAM

A factory was established here *c.*1745 and continued under various partnerships until 1842. Early pottery wares are sometimes marked 'Brameld'. Best known for ornamental porcelain and tea services in rococo style. Invariably all services of this type are attributed to Rockingham, but many are clearly from other factories. Also produced figures and animal models. Rockingham wares are relatively rare and much collected.

RUSKIN

The Ruskin pottery was established by William Howson Taylor in 1898 and closed in 1935. It produced vases with flambé and monochrome glazes. Most sought after are the high fired wares with mottled flambé glazes. Matt monochrome and lustre glazed wares are much less desirable.

Ruskin high fired ware, c.1910

SHELLEY

Wileman & Co. which operated in the period 1872–1925, became known as the Shelley potteries after 1925. Shelley is often taken to be the name of a designer like Clarice Cliff and Susie Cooper, but this is not the case. Best-known wares are the bold Art Deco tea services *c.*1930 and the range of nursery ware designed by Mabel Lucie Attwell.

SPODE-COPELAND

Josiah Spode founded the factory *c.*1770 which was subsequently taken over by Copeland in 1833. The Copeland factory continues to the present day and in the late 19th century, revived the use of the Spode name. Pearlwares, stone china (ironstone) and porcelain were made to a very high standard. The transfer and bat printed wares are particularly collected. Copeland became one of the most important factories in the late 19th century, producing ornamental and tea wares.

WEDGWOOD

Josiah Wegwood founded the factory *c.*1759. The subsequent history is complex, involving various sites in and around Stoke on Trent. Its factory is currently located at a purpose-built site at Barlaston. The range of pottery wares produced by Wedgwood has already been mentioned and the factory was probably the most influential of the 18th-century factories in England. Porcelains were made from the early 19th century onwards but the factory remains famous for its jasperwares (still produced) and latterly its bone china tablewares.

Swansea 'Lysaght' service plate, c.1820

WELSH PORCELAIN

Swansea and Nantgarw were the two main Welsh porcelain factories working in the early 19th century. Wares are finely painted, often with floral subjects and frequently unmarked. Welsh porcelain is much collected and expensive compared to similar work by English factories.

WEMYSS

Scottish pottery established by Robert Heron. Distinctive, boldly painted ware was made under the Wemyss trademark *c.*1900. Many artists later went to work for other factories painting similar wares.

Group of Wemyss wares, c.1900

WORCESTER

The main Worcester factory was established *c.*1751 and has undergone several partnerships to emerge as Royal Worcester today. Notable periods of manufacture in the 19th century include the Flight Barr & Barr partnerships.

Related factories include Chamberlains Worcester and Grainger & Co., Worcester. Wares are generally porcelain and have always developed to follow contemporary trends and fashions. Invariably of high quality, Royal Worcester today is known for its fine tablewares and limited edition figural and animal models.

Royal Worcester figures, c.1900

COLLECTABLE AREAS

Introduction

The following chapter discusses some of the areas not necessarily covered by looking at particular factories, but which constitute some of the most collectable of all ceramic productions. Most of the items looked at in the following sections are readily available to collect. They can be found in antiques shops, junk shops, at antiques fairs and at auction, and a collector can usually form an interesting collection which suits his pocket and, importantly, available display space!

In discussing these areas in more detail (areas which are often overlooked by many general ceramics guides) the aim is to illustrate the breadth and variety of ceramic collecting.

Bear in mind the fact that modern ceramic manufactures are aware of the lure of these collecting areas and are keen to capitalize on them. In almost all of the following fields, items are being produced now, sometimes as direct reproductions, clearly marked, and sometimes as deliberate forgeries or copies. In other cases, manufacturers are keen to make and supply types of 'in demand' wares, hence a proliferation of modern limited editions, royal commemoratives, miniatures and advertising wares. The collector must bear in mind that these pieces are new, readily available and mass-produced. They may, in time, increase in value but meanwhile should be purchased only as a desirable addition to a collection, not as an investment.

Rare Royal Doulton George Robey toby jug, c.1911

Armorials and special commissions

A popular collecting area today is armorial ware. These are pieces which are printed or painted with the coat-of-arms or crest of the family or institution for which they were made.

The most commonly found items of this type are dinner, dessert or teawares. It was common from the early 18th century onwards, when ordering a service, to request the potter add family arms and mottoes, often in celebration of a marriage. Very often the patterns used on such services were standard ones, and it is only the addition of the crest or arms which makes them unique. Some of these services have remained intact within families, but far more were sold off and have gradually become split up over the years.

Such was the popularity of armorial services in the late 18th and early 19th centuries that details of arms would even be sent out to China to be added to the immensely popular export wares. In some cases there might have been a wait of ten years or more before the service was finally sent.

- There are two types of armorial collectors: those who strive to collect as many pieces as possible from a particular service, often family descendants; and those who wish to acquire as many different crests or arms as possible.

- Collectors of armorial porcelain have a dual purpose; not only are they acquiring examples of good-quality ceramics from all periods, but also collecting a part of history, in that the details of the original owners of a piece can often be traced, either by identifying the family crest, or in some cases, by tracking the commission back to the actual factory order books.
- Crested and armorial services were also common for specific clubs and societies. These were sometimes used in the society dining room, or more rarely for a specific dinner, usually with a royal guest. Such pieces often incorporate a royal coat-of-arms.
- Wares related in type to armorial items are those commissioned for specific plates. Most cruise liners

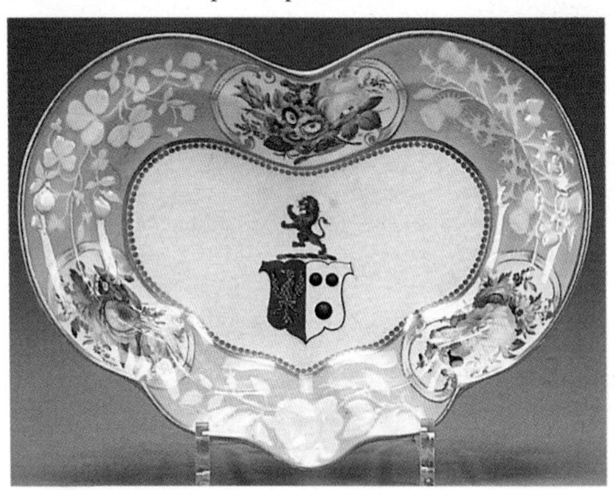

English porcelain armorial dessert dish, c.1825

during the early part of this century had their own services emblazoned with the name of the ship, as did naval ships. Army and Navy officers' messes also had, and still do have specially badged ceramics. As such services become damaged, worn or out-of-date, they would be replaced and sometimes sold off, and became available to add to collections.

English porcelain crested dessert wares, c.1820

Toby and character jugs

Toby jugs were thought to be used as serving jugs to carry ale to the table, but they were more likely to have been, even at that early date, not much more than decorative.

Everybody has heard of the toby jug, essentially a British phenomenon. Although Continental versions exist, these are generally late 19th- and 20th-century copies of their English counterparts, some made for the British market.

The traditional toby jug first appeared in the Staffordshire potteries, *c.*1770. It is not known which potter made the first one, but within a few years they were being produced extensively, a fact clear from the large numbers which survive today, even from this early period. The traditional toby holds a glass or pipe in one hand and a jug or mug of ale in the other. The name toby derives from 'Toper' an old-style word for drinker, and a song about such a drinker, written in 1761 by the Rev. Francis Faulks refers to a character called 'Toby Phillpot'.

Pearlware sailor toby jug, c.1830

Early tobys appear in creamware, and pearlware and were coloured in enamels or Pratt colours. No two seem to be the same and besides the traditional jug there are a host of others in different poses, holding a variety of objects. All have been given names and more commonly seen ones include: 'The Squire' – a figure seated on a corner chair holding a pipe, 'The Snuff Taker' – self explanatory, and 'The Hearty Good Fellow' – standing holding a pipe and jug.

Female tobys were also made, the most commonly seen being 'The Gin Woman', a standing figure and 'Martha Gunn'. Martha Gunn was a character well known in Brighton as a 'bather' who escorted the gentry from their bathing machines into the sea!

This is just a taster of the huge variety of toby jugs which were made right through the late 18th and 19th centuries, the range and charm of which has always appealed to collectors.

The **character jug** is a 20th-century phenomenon, and a spin-off from the toby jug tradition. Character jugs are literally heads, unlike tobys which are always full length figures. The most well known and collected are those made by Royal Doulton from the early part of this century. Many of these are still in production today and there is a ready market for new designs.

Values of most toby and character jugs depend on rarity, with high prices being paid for rare early jugs in good condition, and rare 20th-century jugs, such as the

Royal Doulton jug of Clark Gable which was never put into full production due to the likeness not being approved by the executors of his estate. Early jugs are also sought after by general collectors of early pottery, not just toby collectors.

Initially such jugs were inspired by characters from industry and literature, the characters of Dickens being particularly popular. Modern-day character jugs are often of contemporary figures, and there are jugs of the Beatles, Winston Churchill, Clark Gable and Ronald Reagan, to name but a varied few!

Royal Doulton character jug, 1930s

Hint: To identify a late 18th-century toby from a late 19th-century copy look for the following:

- Good, crisp modelling.
- Arms and jug which are modelled 'in the round' rather than as one with the body.
- Unusual facial details – spots, scars – the uglier the better.
- Feet which overhang the front edge of the base and which can appear hollow underneath.

Finally an important note to end this section: beware of fakes and copies. Traditional toby jugs were mass produced in the late 19th century and these are still quite common today. Also the popularity of character jug collecting and the keenness of collectors to discover unrecorded jugs has led some unscrupulous people to 'create' rarities, which can range from standard jugs with unusual detailing to unrecorded models.

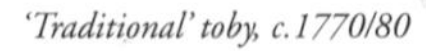

'Traditional' toby, c.1770/80

Animals

Models of animals, large and small, have been popular since the 18th century. While some models of domestic animals were purchased because of their resemblance to favoured pets, models of wild animals were popular because they were previously 'unknown' or 'unseen'. Wild animals first appeared to the general public in engravings, taken from explorers' drawings, and shortly afterwards in the flesh as circus menageries began touring all over Europe in the late 18th and early 19th centuries. Many of these models were cheaply produced and intended as toys for children. Other better quality animal models were intended purely for decoration. The following examples are just a few that a potential collector can hope to find.

Meissen squirrels, c.18th century

MEISSEN

The factory has made animal models almost since the very beginning, ranging from a group of large models designed by Kirchner and Käendler *c.*1730–33, to a 1930s model of an otter in Böttger stoneware by Max Esser. Meissen also made models of different breeds of bird.

STAFFORDSHIRE PORCELAIN

Several English porcelain factories were making models of animals from the mid-18th century onwards. English factories were particularly prolific in the production of animals in the 1830s–40s when popular models included poodles, sheep, cats, rabbits and lions. Rarities in porcelain of this period include tigers, hedgehogs and horses. Some key factories are Chamberlain, Derby, Rockingham and Alcock.

STAFFORDSHIRE POTTERY

Some early pottery animals appear in creamware and pearlware in the 1770s–80s. Often these are quite crisply modelled but were essentially mass produced. In the mid-19th century many Staffordshire potteries were producing animal models alongside their flat back figures. Rarities include camels and elephants, more commonly found are zebras and greyhounds. There are some slipware and Delftware animals known but these are *extremely* rare.

Makers of 20th-century collectable animals include Royal Doulton, Beswick and in Europe, Royal Dux.

Collectors of animal models tend to collect either by breed or type, or by material. Some collect just birds, others dogs, while some will buy only pottery or only porcelain. Early animal models are fairly rare, probably because they were not expensive items at the time, and as toys, were mistreated. Enough, however, do come on the market to make collecting them worthwhile.

Interestingly 'dog' collectors often collect in breeds (just poodles or pugs), while cat collectors collect all cats, regardless.

Staffordshire pottery bear jug, c.1800

Limited editions

The 'limited edition' is essentially a 20th-century phenomenon. The term literally means that the object being purchased has been made in strictly limited quantities.

The term limited edition can be made to imply, particularly in a ceramic manufacturer's promotional literature, that the object is of good quality, collectable and likely to increase in value. Unfortunately, this is rarely the case.

Limited editions are aimed at collectors. Objects are usually marketed in sets or are made to commemorate a special event. Royal Doulton made a series of large limited edition mugs and jugs in the 1930s, and Royal Worcester made several series of animal, bird and fish models, generally limited to editions of 500 or 750, in the 1960s and 1970s. Both these examples are of good quality items, but in both cases the modern price, taking inflation into account, is less than they actually cost new, and these are items made in relatively small numbers. More recent limited editions state that they will be made in a 'limited production run' rather than a specific number of pieces, the limit in this case being the most that the market can bear.

• Modern limited editions, generally speaking, have a very low second-hand value compared to their new cost and should not be purchased with a view to short-, or even long-term investment.

- Some of the very best quality limited edition wares may in time increase in value, but even so, all should be purchased as decoration, not investment.
- The limited edition has become a way for manufacturers to market a modern product, and prospective collectors should try to look through the marketing to the product behind and try to establish for themselves the quality and merit of the product on offer.

Royal Worcester limited edition bull, 1960s

Crested china

For: A collection can be made to suit the pocket of the collector. Common pieces start at a few pounds, a rare piece can be over £1000. The items are small so a collection can be housed easily.
Against: Somewhat repetitive.

Compiling a collection of crested china can be relatively easy and inexpensive, as many of the more common items are readily available at antiques fairs and markets.

Porcelain items bearing the crest of a town or city first began to appear in the late 19th century. With the advent of trains, travel became easier and people began to move more readily around the country. Early pieces of crested china were souvenirs, often made in the shape of a famous historic object from the town or city, and printed or painted with the town arms. The trade soon grew, people began to collect the different shapes and arms and manufacturers made more and more combinations. A peak in production was reached around the time of World War I, with many war souvenirs being made, but the market had all but disappeared by World War II.

Main makers included W.H. Goss, Arcadian China, Carlton Ware and Willow Art China, although Goss pieces are generally the more desirable ones.

Typical crested china souvenirs, c.1900

Novelty wares

This section has been included to give examples of ceramic objects not necessarily covered elsewhere in the book. The term 'novelty' is not ideal, but can be applied to objects where the design or shape is unconventional and not necessarily appropriate for the function! The following are a few examples:

CRUET SETS

Salt, pepper and mustard pots have always been made in a variety of shapes. The Staffordshire potteries made pots in the shape of figures rather like tobys and in the 1920s and 1930s Carlton Ware made a cruet set in the shape of mushrooms, complete with a stand.

COW CREAMERS

Cow-shaped cream jugs first appeared in creamware in the 1760s and became extremely popular (silver cow-shaped cream jugs already existed). Their use died out in the mid-19th century, when it became apparent that their shape made them impossible to clean properly and extremely unhygenic.

Whieldon-type cow creamer, c.1760

Advertising wares

The use of ceramics to advertise a specific product began in the 19th century, and has continued to the present day. Indeed some, such as the ashtrays advertising beer and spirits in pubs, are so familiar that one probably does not think of them as advertising ceramics at all. But that is exactly what they are, and they have many avid collectors.

Advertising wares can be split broadly into two categories: those which advertise the product within them (ginger beer bottles); and those which are made especially to promote a product (those ashtrays again).

Items in the first category include the following: pot lids from pots of hair grease and fish paste, beer bottles and spirit dispensers. Stoneware examples of these were made by Doulton and often advertise a specific brand of spirit.

The second category is probably larger and some of the items harder to find, but include: Pratt printed earthenware plaques advertising Huntley and Palmers biscuits (very rare), jugs, mugs and ashtrays advertising specific wines and spirits.

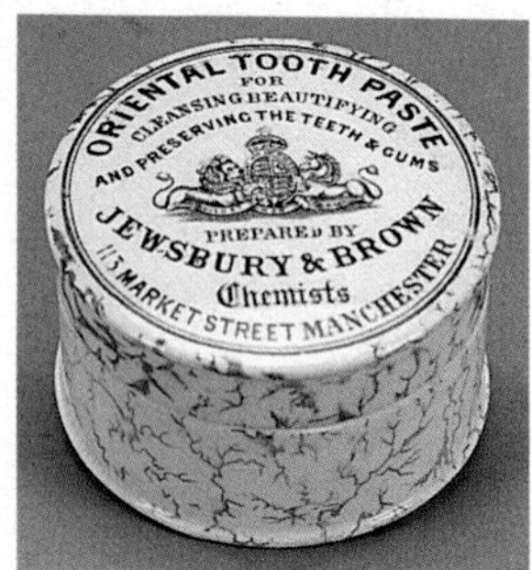

Advertising pot lid, c.1860/80

Other related items include the range of 'Toucan' objects produced by Carlton Ware for Guinness, and wares printed with the Babycham deer.

Ceramics manufacturers also produced signs to be placed in shops to promote their wares; usually these displayed their name, but occasionally also examples of their patterns.

Such has been the enthusiasm of collectors for these items over the last few years that demand has almost outstripped supply, leading some manufacturers to reissue or copy items (notably the Guinness Toucans) or even to create pieces especially for the collectors market. Potential collectors should be aware of this. Advertising wares are interesting things to collect and new promotional items are being issued all the time, making this a constantly developing collecting field.

Modern Belleek advertising plaques

Nursery wares

The earliest wares appeared in the early 19th century and are usually small sized pearlware plates and mugs, printed with educational, moralistic or religious themes.

Nursery wares were made for children, but were traditionally aimed at an adult market, naturally enough as parents were the ones actually buying the items. Frequently the children were too young to understand the designs!

It seems that 19th-century parents clearly intended nursery wares to be instructive rather than decorative. Such wares are generally cheaply made and often unmarked. Plates frequently have plain borders moulded with flowerheads or letters of the alphabet.

By the late 19th century, the range of children's china available had increased. Baby feeding plates with a high rim around the edge and thickly potted, presumably to prevent major damage when hurled to the floor by a frustrated child were popular. Such plates are often chipped or have the central pattern badly rubbed through wear. The patterns are usually brightly coloured, printed and painted and are often accompanied by nursery rhymes.

By the 1920s and 1930s the range of shapes had widened to include cereal bowls and even ceramic handled cutlery. Nearly every major factory produced a range of nursery ware at this period, and the trend was for cute comical subjects rather than overly educational ones. Royal Doulton introduced a range called 'Bunnykins' in the 1930s, designed by Barbara Vernon, which is still current today and included a spin-off range of free standing figures.

The popular illustrator Mabel Lucie Attwell was employed by the Shelley potteries, where her range was based around elves and their activities. Shapes included a teapot in the form of a toadstool house and a cream jug modelled as a saluting elf.

Typical Staffordshire pottery Victorian nursery plate, c.1840

Modern nursery wares are aimed more at the children themselves and subjects are often spin-offs from popular cartoons. Such wares, although mass-produced and sold in large numbers, can soon become quite rare when production ceases due to decline in popularity of the subject, and pieces are damaged or thrown away.

Nursery wares attract collectors because of their subject matter (usually cute, bright and colourful), because of their nostalgic associations with a happy childhood and because there is a wide range affordable and readily available.

A distinction should be made between nursery wares made for children to use and children's wares made for children to play with. The latter are often less collectable and mainly 20th century in date.

Look out for modern wares made in 1930s style, newly made to satisfy strong demand. The type of make and method of decoration, along with signs of use and wear should enable the new collector to make a distinction between old and new.

Crown Ducal baby's plate designed by Charlotte Rhead, 1930s

Commemorative wares

A commonly held belief is that wares made for the coronation of Edward VIII are rare because of his subsequent abdication. This is not the case as a huge amount of ware went into circulation before the announcement. These pieces were then kept as 'rare' treasures, and subsequently survive in large numbers.

Since the earliest slipwares and Delftwares of the 17th century, potteries have been using ceramics to commemorate important events, and since that time such wares have been kept and collected. As with the other collecting areas, later items are readily available, while pre-Victorian pieces are much harder to find. Again there is a strong modern market, making not only cheap souvenirs, but also expensive limited edition items. Commemorative wares fall into several categories:

- Royal – coronations, weddings, births and deaths.
- Political – elections and major political figures.
- Commemoratives of specific events – openings of buildings, bridges, railways.
- Disaster commemoratives – York Minster fire, the Sheffield floods.
- Personal commemoratives – births, weddings, christenings. Such items often name a particular person and date.

By far the most widely produced and collected are royal commemoratives, the earliest being Delftware plates made in the reign of Charles II. Pieces are

The most affordable modern commemoratives are lowly pottery coffee mugs, which have been issued since the 1980s to commemorate and advertise a huge range of events. These are now beginning to be snapped up by collectors with the rarer ones selling for many times their new price.

comparatively rare up to and including the coronation of Queen Victoria. During her reign, commemorating events in ceramic became more popular and included the births and marriages of her many children and the death of Prince Albert.

Huge amounts of ware was made for Victoria's Golden and Diamond Jubilees in 1887 and 1897 respectively and all royal events after this date are widely commemorated. Some particular pieces are rare and desirable but generally values are low for the commonly made mugs, cups and saucers.

Rare Jacobite commemorative salt-glazed mug, c.1745/50

Miniatures

Very small miniatures were probably made for dolls houses; with a few exceptions (notably the vases made by Royal Worcester for Queen Mary's dolls house) these tend to be of fairly low quality.

Miniature items have a popular modern collecting appeal, particularly because space is a prime consideration in small modern homes. A miniature, strictly speaking, is a smaller than normal-sized object made as a direct replica of a larger one. Many factories made these in the 19th and 20th centuries and they seem to have been purely decorative.

It has sometimes been suggested that miniatures were made as travellers' samples and, although in some

rare instances this may be the case, the general feeling is that most were not. Similarly, some miniatures were made as toys for children, but given the delicacy of some which survive, this cannot always have been the case.

Due to their collectability, the price of miniatures is always surprisingly high, compared with that of their larger counterparts, and good quality pieces are surprisingly expensive and hard to find. Collectable miniatures include:

- Royal Crown Derby pieces painted with bright *Imari* patterns, including miniature teapots, cups, flat irons, coal scuttles, shovels, vases and trays.
- Transfer printed pearlware dinner services of the 1820s–30s.
- Miniature creamware dinner services from the turn of the 18th century.
- Ornamental miniatures by Minton and Rockingham from the 1830s–40s, including tiny teapots and candlesticks.
- Miniature Dresden cups and saucers painted with panels of figures and flowers.

Royal Worcester, Royal Crown Derby and other miniatures, all under 2in high (5cm)

Other collecting areas

There are many other collecting areas that remain unexplored here, but the following two are worth mentioning:

POT LIDS

Lids from fish paste and cosmetic cream pots printed either to advertise the product inside or with colourful all-over views and scenes were made in the second half of the 19th century and are widely collected. Most are circular and are often mounted in wood frames. The patent colour printed process by which they were decorated has already been mentioned; this enabled the lids to be printed with a huge variety of contemporary or nostalgic subjects. Scenes include views of Pegwell Bay, Kent, famous for its shrimps, images of politicians and royalty, reproductions of famous paintings, and animal, bird and plant subjects. A series made to

contain bear grease for men's hair shows different scenes of bears in the wild or in anthropomorphic poses.

FAIRINGS

Cheaply made German novelty ornaments dating from the turn of the century were made in series, reflecting contemporary life, and usually bore a gilt title. Often the subjects are humorous or satirical. The most important maker was the Elbogen factory. Their pieces bear an impressed mark of an arm holding a sword within a shield. Collectors should be aware of copies made in the 1960s when fairings were particularly popular. These often tend to be lighter in weight than the originals.

Colour-printed pot lids and mug, c.1860

COMPENDIUM 

Dating

It is always interesting to try to establish the date of manufacture of an item, but this can sometimes be difficult, particularly if there are no marks underneath to use as a guide. Very often it is a matter of looking at the item itself to see what clues it provides. The following pointers should help.

- Look for any marks and use a comprehensive marks book to look them up. The notes given in the marks section of this book should be helpful. Not all marks should be taken literally!
- Look at the body of the ware. Does it fall into any of the categories discussed in previous chapterss?
- Look at the typeface of any marks or inscriptions. Does it look modern? Continental?
- Consider the shape. Is the piece angular and modern, stylized and sinuous, classical or Rococo?
- What type of decoration does it have? Printed or painted? When was this style of decoration popular?
- Very early items can be thermoluminescence-tested for age. This is expensive and only helpful in limited cases.
- Bear in mind that deliberate fakes and forgeries exist. Use a combination of the above indicators to arrive at a final decision.

• Try to work out who may have owned the item if it is a family piece. Allow approximately 20–25 years per generation.
• If defeated, take the object to an experienced dealer or auctioneer. This type of advice is usually free and can be very helpful.

Meissen Harlequin, 20th century

Fakes and forgeries

As earlier chapters have explained, copies of designs on ceramics began in Europe in the 17th century, with the Dutch Delft potters copying Chinese designs on their wares. Today, these pieces are not considered fakes or forgeries, so it must first be established what is meant by a fake or forgery.

- To fake is to alter an object with the intent of hiding its true appearance or origins.
- To forge is to create an entirely new object in the style of another, usually older or more valuable piece.

As it has been noted, ceramic shapes and designs have always been copied, and to attempt to try to list all the different factories and wares would be impossible and not particularly helpful. However, it is possible to give a few hints on how to identify a fake, and give some indication of 19th-century and modern reproductions which the reader is likely to come across.

A typical Samson bowl, in Chinese 18th-century style

The best known 19th-century forger was a man called Samson working in Paris in the last quarter of that century. He is so well-known and made such good copies that his work is collected in its own right today.

Samson specialized in making replacements for services and broken pairs of figures or vases, mostly in porcelain but also some tin-glazed wares. He used fake marks including gold anchors on Chelsea-style figures, fake red painted Derby marks, Chinese seal marks and many Continental marks, as well as his own distinctive interlaced S mark. Besides replacements, he made decorative items intended to deceive and even today it is sometimes difficult to detect a Samson copy of an 18th-century figure. The main give-away is usually not the shape or decoration but the body itself, which is usually a typically French hard paste porcelain and quite unlike that used by the English and German factories he was copying.

Other areas where 19th- and early 20th-century reproductions occur are in Italy with 19th-century copies of early maiolica; in Staffordshire with copies of creamware and 'Whieldon-type' ware made *c.*1900; and in France with many 19th-century Paris or Limoges items bearing fake Sèvres interlaced 'L' marks.

Distinctive marks used by factories other than the originals included the Meissen crossed swords, the crowned N of Naples (Capodimonte) and the shield mark of Vienna.

Detail of typical Samson mark

Reproductions or forgeries appearing on the market this century include copies of Staffordshire 'flat-back' figures, often with fake crazing; also reproductions of maiolica and ironstone wares. With all three it is the body which gives the piece away rather than shape or decoration. Fakes of collectable Art Deco pieces such as Clarice Cliff are also being made.

Always be suspicious of items which seem too good to be true. They may be a bargain but are more likely to be wrong. Take into account the known provenance as well as the type of body, decoration and shape. Look at an object and use common sense. The more pieces you look at the more you will get a feel for the right object. Look at the wear and condition. Is it consistent with the apparent age?

A last point to consider – the object is 'right' but has been tampered with to make it more valuable. Decoration and detail can be added at a later date to make an item more desirable. Wear can also be added to make an item appear older. This is often the case with very new reproductions which are sometimes even painted with a film of grey paint to make them appear as if they have been around a long time gathering dust.

Deliberately aged Italian maiolica vase, 20th century

Condition, care and restoration

The condition of a ceramic piece is of great importance and should certainly be taken into account if a purchase is being considered. Damage, in its many forms, can strongly affect the value of a piece, and may worsen, eventually affecting its appearance as well. The following points look at what forms damage can take, factors which affect condition, and restoration of damaged items.

Damage and condition

- Chips are usually more noticeable than cracks, but are self-contained and can be more easily restored.
- Cracks can worsen. Be aware of highly decorated items where cracks may be difficult to spot. An uncracked porcelain plate or bowl should ring when tapped on the rim. If the sound is flat or dull it may indicate a hidden crack.
- Losses, such as hands missing from figures, can be difficult to restore well as the restorer must have an example of a complete original to copy.
- Flaking of enamels and surface wear can be as detrimental to

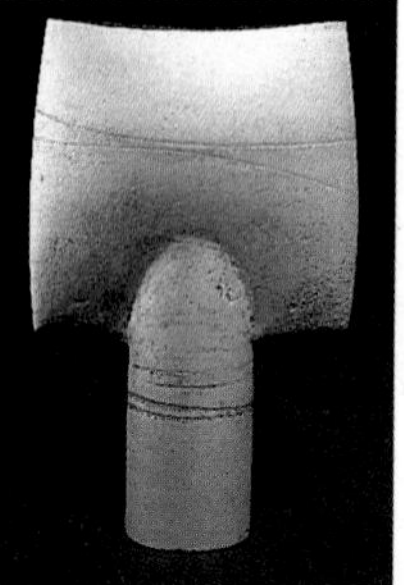

Damaged Hans Coper 'spade' vase, c.1970

price as cracks and chips. If the decorative appearance of a piece is lost, its value will be reduced too.

- Crazing – minute fractures in the glaze caused by it shrinking at a different rate to the body when an item leaves the kiln – is not, strictly speaking, damage, but should be considered when examining the condition of a piece. Heavy crazing can be disfiguring. (On some monochrome glazed wares crazing is deliberate.)
- Similarly, damage done to a piece during firing (cracks and glaze faults) can also affect value.

English plate, c.1820, with chipped rim

Care

- Most porcelains with a lead glaze can be washed in warm soapy water. However, crazing, cracks and chips can allow water to be absorbed by the body, taking with it dirt which can cause stains.
- If in doubt, consult a restorer who can advise on the best way of cleaning a piece, as well as giving advice regarding repair.
- Avoid dishwashers. With regular use these will eventually fade even the most modern wares.
- Ceramics should not be subjected to extremes of heat and cold as this can cause expansion or contraction of the body, leading to the sudden appearance of cracks
- Avoid sprung plate hangers which stretch across the backs of plates. These can put undue stress on the rim, causing chips and cracks. Plastic covered ones are better, but still not recommended.

Dresden inkstand, c.1900

Royal Doulton stoneware vase, c.1890

Restoration

HOW TO DETECT RESTORATION

- The restored area will feel warmer to touch than the rest of the piece and also softer if scratched with a hard object. The original glaze is fired hard like glass, whereas restoration is, in effect, a layer of filler and paint.
- Hold porcelain items up to the light. Areas of restoration are not translucent and will be dark.
- Examine closely for changes in colour and style of painting. On crazed earthenware items the restorer will have had to add painted crazing to the restored area. This usually looks quite different.
- Look closely at the edges of plates or bowls. Restoration is usually easier to spot right on the rim.
- Ultraviolet light will show up restoration with a purple glow.

- Professional restoration can improve the appearance of an item, as well as stabilizing damage. Beware of poor quality obvious restoration.
- Restoration will not necessarily increase the value of a piece.
- Old restoration

An apparently perfect Belleek tea kettle

can take the form of metal rivets. These do give a piece 'character', but they can rust and cause further damage.

- Beware of restoration which changes the original appearance of a piece. Look out for new heads on old bodies, elements missing from figure groups, extensive overspraying or overpainting and retouching of flaked enamels.

Strong light shows the restored area

Price

Before buying or selling an item or starting to collect, it is a good idea to have a look around shops, fairs and auctions for similar items to get a feel for the market. The following is a list of various factors which may affect price, and which may only be apparent if you know the market well.

- **Condition:** Is the item damaged or worn? Or is it a really good example, in mint condition?
- **Collectablity:** Some items are far more fiercely collected than others, and collecting fashions change, making prices go up and down.
- **Usefulness:** Could the piece be used?
- **Size:** Very large items are not necessarily worth more than smaller ones, since they can be too big for modern homes. Similarly, miniatures are extremely popular and, relative to size, highly priced.
- **Rarity:** Is it a rare pattern or shape, or a combination of both?
- **Location:** Where you buy can affect price. A dealer may be more expensive than buying at auction, but the piece may be well restored, or just the one you are looking for.
- **Age:** Not a factor which usually affects price. All the above are far more relevant.

Meissen vase, c.1870, approximately 1.5 metres high

Forming a collection

The following are a few points to consider when trying to decide what to collect or how to develop an existing collection.

- Decide whether the collection will be the work of one particular factory, one period, one shape or a particular type of ware. Collecting a specific era or factory should

Worcester cup and saucer, c.1770

enable you to gain a detailed knowledge of that field, whereas collecting a shape or style of ware will mean that knowledge will be broader and more general.

- Collect for pleasure, not for profit. Trying to buy well is one thing, aiming to make a profit is more difficult.
- Try to match what you collect to available display space. It is much more satisfying to be able to see the collection than to have it packed away in boxes.

Samson mug in Worcester style, late 19th century

- Try to suit your pocket. Attempting to collect what you cannot really afford will lead to the purchase of damaged or poor examples, disappointment at pieces priced out of your range and inevitably a small collection!
- Try to buy the best examples possible, items in good condition or with unusual designs.
- Prune the collection. It may be impossible to sell the first piece purchased, but as your knowledge of the ware increases, some items will become less interesting or relevant to the collection.
- Base the collection around items which attract you or

Crown Ducal Charlotte Rhead charger, 1930s

pieces which have been inherited. Most collectors have a reason for collecting.

- Join the relevant club or society if there is one.

Where to find out more

The following may be helpful sources of information and advice for identifying objects and increasing knowledge.

AUCTIONEERS

Most auctioneers will give free valuations on objects, and the larger salerooms will have ceramic experts who will usually identify and date a piece, all without charge.

LIBRARIES

Most large public libraries have a good selection of books on antiques. The trick is to know where to start. Hopefully this book will help!

DEALERS

Established general antiques shops will usually give general advice. Specialist dealers may be able to help with identification.

COLLECTORS' GROUPS AND SOCIETIES

There are many of these, usually set up by enthusiasts. Some publish magazines where pieces are advertised, and seminars and meetings are arranged where knowledge can be exchanged. Specialist books often give details of relevant societies; alternatively museums and auctioneers may be able to supply addresses.

LECTURES

Clubs and societies arrange lectures, as do groups such as NADFAS. Museums also run ceramic lecture courses.

MUSEUMS

Most museums run an identification service. The Victoria and Albert Museum, London and the City Museum and Art Gallery, Stoke-on-Trent, both have strong ceramic collections.

Prattware jug, c.1790

Where to buy

The following are the most likely places to buy ceramics, along with some advantages and disadvantages. With any of these, the buyer must use his or her discretion; there will always be as many overpriced items as there are bargains!

AUCTIONS

• **For:** Trade prices, pieces can usually be bought cheaper than from shops or fairs. Some salerooms will indicate damage and restoration and will accurately describe items. If items are found not to be as catalogued, some rooms will take them back.
• **Against:** Lots may contain more than just the items you want. Some people are put off by the thought of having to bid; more on that later!

SPECIALIST DEALERS, SHOPS AND FAIRS

• **For:** Pieces are well presented. A rapport can be built up and many dealers operate a finding service. A good dealer will buy back items and perhaps do 'part exchanges'. They offer a wide choice of the desired items.
• **Against:** Prices can be higher.

GENERAL DEALERS, ANTIQUES FAIRS AND CAR BOOT SALES

• **For:** Wide choice at many venues throughout the country. Specialist knowledge may result in the purchase of a bargain. They offer the fun of the search.
• **Against:** Restoration or damage may not be disclosed. Beware reproductions.

CLASSIFIED ADVERTISEMENTS, NEWSPAPERS AND COLLECTORS' MAGAZINES

- **For:** Dealing directly with the private vendor or collector. Specialist magazines may have a wide choice of items. 'Wants' can also be advertised.
- **Against:** Sometimes it is difficult to fix a price with a fellow collector.

Staffordshire pearlware 'Willow pattern' dish, c.1820

Buying and selling at auction

Auctions can be daunting for the newcomer but many buyers soon find they enjoy the fun of the chase for a particular piece.

BUYING

Sales are usually 'on view' two or three days beforehand and most salerooms produce a catalogue of some type, with guide estimates. Advice can also be asked for in respect of condition of the piece and presale interest.

- View the item and fix a price. This is important so as not to get carried away later.
- Bidding can be done in person, by leaving a written bid with the auctioneer, or (less usually) by telephone.
- If the bid is left with the auctioneers (on commission) they will treat this as a maximum price and try to purchase the piece as cheaply as other bids allow.
- Bidding in person is fun. Do not worry about inadvertently buying the wrong lot, a good auctioneer will know the difference between a scratch of the nose and a real bid!
- Once paid for, the item is yours. It is as simple as that.

SELLING

Items need to be brought into the auctioneers in plenty of time for items to be included in a catalogue. Estimates will be suggested and a reserve or minimum price will usually be fixed. Upon sale of the item, the auctioneer takes a percentage commission as a selling fee.

• There is often no charge for lots which fail to sell, but do check first.

• Payment is made once the auctioneers have been paid, ten to 35 days after the sale.

Meissen topographical vase, c.1840

Collections

Following is a list of a few museums and collections in Europe which are worth visiting for their ceramic collections.

ENGLAND

Fitzwilliam Museum, Cambridge
Victoria & Albert Museum, London
City Museum & Art Gallery, Stoke-on-Trent
Dyson Perrins Museum, Worcester
Sir Henry Doulton Gallery, Royal Doulton, Stoke-on-Trent
Wedgwood Museum, Barlaston, Staffordshire
Minton Museum, Stoke-on-Trent
Spode Museum, Stoke-on-Trent
Coalport China Works, Coalport, Shropshire
Ashmolean Museum, Oxford

EUROPE

Musée Ceramique de la Manufacture Nationale, Sèvres, France
Musée du Louvre, Paris
Rijksmuseum, Amsterdam

Most Continental towns where ceramic manufacture has been significant will have good collections of native wares.

Westerwald German stoneware ewer, 18th century

Marks

INTRODUCTION

The following pages list the marks of the specific factories discussed in previous chapters and some marks which collectors may commonly come across. This section is by no means comprehensive but should be a helpful starting point. When trying to identify or date an object by the mark underneath, the following pointers will be helpful:

- England, or the country of origin incorporated into a mark usually indicates a date after 1891.
- 'Made in' usually appears after *c.*1920.
- Painted numerals underneath a piece are usually a pattern code, not a date.
- Moulded or impressed numerals underneath are usually a shape code.
- Marks incorporating addresses may be retailers' rather than makers' marks.
- Dates incorporated into marks are misleading (Coalport AD1750). These usually relate to the date of foundation of the factory or the date of introduction of the original version of the pattern.
- Be aware that makers in the late 19th and 20th centuries gave patterns names which allude to illustrious factories or patterns ('Chelsea' or 'Dresden').
- Many 20th-century Staffordshire factories used similar words in their trademarks ('New Chelsea', 'Old Hall'). Such traditional-style names gave a implication of quality to the ware.

- Terms such as 'bone china', '22ct gold' and 'hand-painted' were used only in this century.
- With Continental ceramics, look out for 'Eneret' and 'Geschutz', both of which mean patent and were used from the late 19th century onwards.
- Early pieces often have only the name of a factory or maker impressed or printed underneath.
- Look out for marks in unusual places, inside the rim of vases, on the backs of figures, and signatures and monograms incorporated into the decoration.

Detail of misleading Coalport mark, used c.1900

STUDIO POTTERY MARKS

Seal mark of Hans Coper.

Seal mark of St Ives Pottery and personal seal of Bernard Heach.

Seal mark of Lucie Rie.

BRITISH AND IRISH MARKS

ADAMS
ESTBD 1657
TUNSTALL,
ENGLAND

W. Adams & Co. Printed mark used *c.*1900. Earlier and later versions exist with confusing establishment dates.

J. Aynsley & Sons (1864–). Printed mark used from 1891.

Belleek Pottery, Ireland (1863–). Early mark in black, printed or impressed. Ireland added later.

Bishop & Stonier (1891–1939). Printed mark.

Brown Westwood Moore & Co. (1861–1904). Printed mark.

Burmantofts, Leeds (1882–1904). Impressed mark.

Carter Stabler and Adams, Poole Pottery (1921–). Early impressed mark.

Coalport China Works, Shropshire (late 18th century–present day). Printed mark used *c.*1881–1939.

Susie Cooper, Burslem (1929–66), later part of Wedgwood group. Printed mark 1930s.

Crown Staffordshire Porcelain Co. Ltd (1889–). Printed mark used after 1930.

Derby Porcelain Co. Later, Royal Crown Derby. Various partnerships. Painted mark used *c.*1782–1825 (*c.*1800–25 in red enamel).

Royal Doulton. Printed mark used *c.*1902–22 and *c.*1927–36. Many other marks exist.

George Jones & Sons Ltd (*c.*1864-1907). Crescent Pottery (*c.*1907–51). Printed or impressed mark.

Keeling & Co. (1886–1936). Printed mark.

G.M. & C.J. Mason (1813-30). Printed mark. Used later by Ashworths.

William Moorcroft (1913–). Signature mark used 1913–1920s. Later marks impressed.

Myott, Son & Co. Ltd (1898–). Various printed marks.

Arthur, J. Wilkinsons Ltd. Newport Pottery. Printed mark *c.*1928–1950s.

Pilkingtons Tile & Pottery Co. Ltd (*c.*1893–1957). Impressed mark.

Rockingham Works (*c.*1745–1842). Printed mark *c.*1826–30 (in red), *c.*1830–42 (in puce).

Shelley Potteries Ltd (*c.*1925–). Formerly Wileman & Co. Printed mark 1925–50s.

Josiah Spode (*c.*1770–1833). Later Copeland & Garrett. Printed mark *c.*1805–30. Similar mark used *c.*1900 by Copeland.

Wedgwood & Co. (*c.*1860–1965). (NB: not Josiah Wedgwood). Printed mark.

Josiah Wedgwood, *c.*18th century–present day. Printed mark used *c.*1878–.

Wiltshaw & Robinson (*c.*1890–1957 and later). Early and later printed marks.

Worcester. Various partnerships and marks. Barr Flight and Barr (*c.*1807–13). Royal Worcester (1862–). Printed and impressed marks.

CONTINENTAL MARKS

Attwasser (1845–1918). Printed mark.

Berlin, Royal factory (1763–). Printed and impressed marks.

Bonn, Germany. Franz Anton Mehlem (1755–20th century). Printed mark *c.*1900.

Copenhagen Royal Works (1755–). Printed mark *c.*1900–.

Dresden, Germany. Similar marks used by several factories *c.*1890–.

Jacob Petit, France (*c.*1834–). Underglaze-blue mark *c.*1834–62.

Rosenthal, Germany (*c.*1897–). Printed marks.

Ludwigsburg, Germany (1758–1824). Underglaze-blue mark (much copied).

Meissen (*c.*1708–). Underglaze-blue marks.
1. Academic period 1763–73.

2. Marcolini period 1774–1814.

3. Later mark 19th–20th centuries.

Naples. Mark used by numerous factories in Germany and Italy, 18th–20th centuries.

Zsolnay Pecs (1862–). Printed and moulded mark.

Underglaze-blue marks used by Sitzendorf and Plaue, Germany. Late 19th–early 20th centuries.

Samson, Paris (*c.*1873–early 20th century). Faker who also used copies of various other factory marks.

Sèvres (1756–). Painted mark, much copied in 19th century.

Vienna (*c.*1718–). Shield mark in underglaze-blue, much copied.

Michael Ambrose Cardew (b1901). Personal mark used on slipware and pottery.

Suggested reading

There are many books – too numerous to mention here – which specialize in the products of individual factories. Below are a few invaluable general books which will provide more helpful information.

English Blue and White Porcelain of the 18th Century, Bernard Watney. Faber & Faber. London, 1973.

British Pottery. An Illustrated Guide, Geoffrey A. Godden. Barrie & Jenkins. London, 1974.

British Porcelain. An Illustrated Guide, Geoffrey A. Godden. Barrie & Jenkins. London, 1974.

European Ceramic Art, W. B. Honey. Faber & Faber. London, 1952.

Sotheby's Concise Encyclopaedia of Porcelain, Ed. David Battie. Conran Octopus. London, 1994.

Encyclopaedia of British Pottery & Porcelain Marks, Geoffrey A. Godden. Barrie & Jenkins. London, 1964.

Directory of European Porcelain, L. Danckert. NAG Press. London, 1981.

English Porcelain Animals of the 19th Century, D. G. Rice. Antique Collectors Club. Woodbridge, 1984.

The Book of Meissen, R. E. Rontgen. Schiffer Publishing. Pennsylvania, 1984.

World Ceramics, Ed. R.J. Charleston. Hamlyn. London, 1977.

British Studio Ceramics in the 20th Century, R. Rice & C. Gowing. Barrie & Jenkins. London, 1983.

Staffordshire Portrait Figures, P. D. Gordon Pugh. Antique Collectors Club, 1970.

English Earthenware Figures 1740–1840, Pat Halfpenny. Antique Collectors Club, 1991.

Royal Worcester jug, c.1890

Glossary

Arita: Area of Japan from which much porcelain, including *kakiemon* and *Imari* wares were exported.

Artificial porcelain: Another term for soft paste porcelain.

Basketweave: Relief moulded pattern with woven appearance.

Baluster: Narrowing swollen shape, resembling supports of a balustrade, with the upper and lower parts cylindrical or slightly flaring.

Blanc de chine: Term used to describe white Chinese porcelain from Fukien Province, copied in Europe.

Blue scale: Pattern of overlapping scale motifs, usually blue and underglaze, and used commonly at Worcester. Scale patterns can be enamelled in various colours.

Bocage: Leafy tree-like support or background to figure groups. Sometimes floral.

Campana vase: Thistle-shaped vase raised on a spreading foot and narrow stem, the shoulders set with loop handles.

Celadon: Name for a Chinese pale green glaze, copied in Europe.

Charger: Large serving plate, often circular or oval.

Chinoiserie: European decoration inspired by Oriental sources, particularly China.

Comport: Form of dessert dish on a stem base, popular in the 19th century.

Cover: Lid. The term lid tends to be used when only when the cover is hinged, and then not always.

Encrusted: Term used to describe profuse applied decoration, usually flowerheads and fruit.

Finial: Ornament at the top of a vessel.

Flambé: Term used to describe a glaze, usually red in colour.

Foot-rim: the rim projecting underneath a vessel or plate on which it rests

Gadrooning: Term and style taken from silversmithing to describe a beaded or fluted border pattern.

In the white: Term used to describe undecorated porcelain.

Jardinière: Large ornamental vessel for growing plants, or disguising a plant pot.

Knop: As finial, but specifically used for the finial on top of a cover.

Maguette: Sculptor's small preliminary model in wax, clay, etc.

Monochrome: Term used to described a single-colour glaze, or single-colour enamel painted decoration.

Ormolu: Gilt bronze. Mounts on porcelain are often ormolu, or a cheap gilt metal imitation.

Osier pattern: Relief moulded basketweave pattern.

Powder-blue: Cobalt blue applied underglaze in powder form to give a distinctive mottled dark blue colour.

Prunus: Plum blossom.

Reticulated: Pattern of interlacing lines or pierced work which forms a net or web.

Shards (sherds): Broken fragments of porcelain or pottery such as those found on excavated sites.

Tazza: Type of ornamental cup or vase having a large, flat, shallow bowl which rests on a stem base or a low foot; it may be with or without handles.

Tree and well: Pattern of indentations on a meat plate intended to allow gravy to drain off (resembling a tree).

Tureen: Serving dish for soup (if large enough) or sauce (if smaller). Usually with cover, stand and a ceramic ladle.

Well: Central indented part of a plate or dish.

Index